Clap One Hand

Clap One Hand
for the
Big Bang

Ian Pullen

FINDHORN
Press

British Library Cataloguing-in-Publication Data.
A catalogue record for this book is available
from the British Library.

Set in Palatino by Findhorn Press
Cover illustration © Lizzie Pullen 1994
Author photograph by Findhorn Foundation Visual Arts
Cover design by Posthouse Printing
Printed and bound by Cromwell Press Ltd,
Melksham, England

Published by
Findhorn Press
The Park, Findhorn,
Forres IV36 0TZ, Scotland
01309-690582

Contents

About the title . . . .

Clap One Hand . . . .

Zen Buddhism uses a series of unsolvable riddles as foci
for meditation. These are called koans and one of the most
famous is 'What is the sound of one hand clapping?'
Although many western people use the logical mind to
produce an answer to the question posed by this koan,
they miss the point: any answer is irrelevant — meditation as a way to move beyond the confines of the
mind is all that matters.

. . . . for the Big Bang

In 1948 the astrophysicist Gamov wrote a thesis on the
LeMaître theory concerning the creation of the universe.
He called the primal explosion from which Abbé LeMaître
postulated that the universe originated, 'The Big Bang'.
This is one of the most popular scientific theories currently
in vogue concerning the origin of our universe and the
phrase 'The Big Bang' has become part of common usage.

Chapter 1

Starting on a Journey

The universe is full of mysteries and miracles. Really big mysteries such as the origin of God and just how many stars there are in the sky, and unremarkable little mysteries such as where ballpoint pens vanish to and why the telephone always seems to stop ringing just before you manage to answer it. Miracles which range from the changing of water into wine to the occasional arrival of the 8.42 train on time. Even science is full of mysteries: such as what gravity is really all about. It's all very well for physicists to make clever statements such as 'matter attracts matter' or 'space is bent', but such comments aren't really explanations. The average person remains just as unknowledgeable about the force that keeps us pinned to the earth as he or she was before such enigmatic observations were made.

Perhaps the biggest mysteries are centred around the questions of who we are and what we are doing in this universe; the ultimate mystery might well be why we exist (or think we exist) at all. A popular song of the 1960s asked, 'What's it all about, Alfie?'; and, although the song was referring primarily to Alfie's sexual urges, the general question, 'What's it all about?' is one we all ask at one time or another concerning our place in the universe. We ask it about God, and occasionally we look up at the night sky with its myriad twinkling stars and ask it about the universe — whether it really goes on in space and time for ever.

To find the answer to these questions, we need to take a journey. Not by rocket to the moon; not even to the local library or church; but a journey both inwards and outwards starting from the Self. This is a journey of discovery; to find out how we relate to the world around us and what the universe we travel through actually consists of. Many books have already been written on these subjects, from both spiritual and scientific points of view. But this one is different because it combines these two apparently diverse concepts and describes a system which is understandable to both scientists and laymen.

Most of us are different from what we imagine ourselves to be; similarly the universe is unbelievably different from what we have been told by the majority of priests, gurus and scientists. In the course of the journey we are about to undertake we will unearth a lot more about its mysteries and miracles, and we will learn a great deal more about ourselves at all levels. This will not only make Life easier to live, but will make it even more enjoyable and fascinating too.

Of the books already available which talk about awareness, mysticism and spiritual matters, very few take into account scientific opinion. In fact, many of them are so muddled and unscientific that they raise the scientist's eyebrows to vanishing point. If ideas about our destiny are to be truly acceptable, they must embrace the viewpoints of us all, including atheists, religious fanatics, scientists and simpletons. Therefore the following pages include references to Relativity, Quantum theory, quarks, the speed of light, and other well known and not so well known scientific conjectures. These references are easy for non-technical people to follow. Likewise the sections which discuss arcane aspects of 'the Mysteries' are written in simple English instead of using lots of Sanskrit terms, so that those with scientific leanings will be comfortable with these perspectives too.

To illustrate the point about our being different from what we think we are, let me tell you a story about a tiger and a goat. Once upon a time (starting as all good stories should) a tiger cub was abandoned by its mother, and found by a passing herd of goats. It was adopted by one of the nannygoats who had recently lost her kid, and grew up amongst the goats believing itself a goat. It made goat noises,

ate the bark of trees, and ran away whenever predators
appeared. It was content with its goat-like existence, or at
least as content as any permanently wary and continually
frightened animal could be. Then, one dreamy day, it was a
little slow in running and was caught by an old tiger. It
stood trembling in the grass waiting to be devoured at a
gulp; but the old tiger just looked at it quizzically and asked,
'What are you doing here with all these goats?' The tiger
cub, its eyes tightly shut, trembled even more and made
frightened goat noises. 'Stop those silly noises,' growled the
old tiger, 'and pull yourself together.' 'I can't help it' stut-
tered the cub. 'I'm a goat and you're going to eat me. I'm
very frightened.' 'Oh, are you indeed!' muttered the tiger.
He picked the cub up gently with his teeth, padded across to
a nearby pond and plonked it down at the edge. 'Now,' he
said,'what do you see in the water?' The cub continued to
stand there shivering with its eyes tightly shut. 'Open your
eyes and LOOK!' roared the tiger; which so terrified the cub
that its eyes snapped open and, wonder of wonders, it saw
in the still water a very handsome young tiger staring back
at it. 'See,' said the old tiger in a gentle growl, 'you are not a
goat at all. You are a tiger. Never pretend to be a goat again.
Go off and act like a tiger from now on.' And the young ex-
goat, revelling in its new-found freedom, bounded off practising growling noises.

Most of us spend the greater part of our lives believing
we are goats and not acknowledging our 'tigerness'. We
become used to assuming that the world is a 'dangerous'
place and being frightened by this, that , or the other. But all
the time we are going around with the herd we are actually
missing countless opportunities to look into the water and
discover that we are really tigers. Whatever our age, whatever our sex, whatever our work, whatever 'sins' we have
been guilty of, whatever deficiencies we feel we have,
behind the façades we have each made for ourselves, there is
a beautiful tiger waiting to be discovered and acknowl-

edged. In truth, each one of us knows all there is to know about both ourselves and the universe; and all the learning we undertake is actually a process of recognising that we have this in-built knowledge. It is a process of becoming more *aware*. Logic, fear, plus a lack of love for others and self, puts a mist over the mirror of the pool.

So a major part of the purpose of our journey — in its early stages at any rate — is to find the right pool in which to see the real Self by blowing away the mist. Then, when we see our true reflection, we have to recognise it for what it really is. Generally, we see what we expect to see. Thus, although a tiger looks back at us from the pool, we still see a goat. It often takes the intervention of a Master to shock us into acknowledging our Reality. The essence of that Reality is that we are inherently and unalterably godly.

In the course of our travels we will be looking at — amongst other things — alchemy and astrology, deities and demons, poltergeists and the paranormal. These are all possible parts of the universe and are just as 'real' as the molecules, electromagnetic fields and gravitons we shall also be looking at. They may not be as easy to express mathematically, nor will they be capable of repetitious demonstration in a laboratory; but someone who has had a poltergeist-propelled saucepan whiz past their head will only be too pleased to assure you that these phenomena are *real*.

Maybe you 'believe' in them and maybe you don't. Maybe you haven't really thought about them at all. It doesn't really matter because, hopefully, you will have a totally different set of beliefs by the time you reach the end of this book. The universe is in a continuous state of change, and our journey will be more enjoyable if we also stay open to change. Beliefs and disbeliefs are simply markers along the way. Ideally, they should change as the journey progresses. When I was six, I believed all that my teachers told me; by the time I was fourteen I suspected that they were nearly always wrong. Now I think that they were just as confused as the rest of us, and gave out a mixture of fact and fable according to contemporary thought.

So, for the time being, acknowledge that you have changeable beliefs and disbeliefs. Then, put them to one side, study the descriptions and arguments in the following pages, and discover a fascinating new universe unfolding before your eyes.

One of the pleasures of being a human being with both a logical mind and spiritual feelings is the capability of re-appraising accepted viewpoints in the light of fresh mental and intuitive input. Once we stop saying '. . . . but I might be wrong', part of the zest of life goes missing. There is no longer any room for new ideas, new perspectives on the world, new experiences in which to revel. This book contains my ideas and feelings, ... and they might be wrong. However, they help me to make God and the universe more enjoyable and more exciting. They help me on my particular journey. As the years go by, my spiritual and worldly views have changed, and they will go on changing. What is written here is just one set of impressions which have helped me along my path of continuous discovery. Each day brings new perspectives and new delights. By sharing some of them with you, my fellow travellers, it may be that you too will discover new riches to enjoy as you move along your own particular path.

One of the many things we will be examining during our journey is the structure of time because this is one of the biggest mysteries of all. We live our lives totally immersed in this strange effect and it governs much of what we do and think, so it would be a Good Thing to find out more about it. Is there such a thing as the 'future', or is it just repetitions of the past seen from different perspectives? Is there such a thing as the 'past' or is that just a distorted view of the 'present'? Is the speed of light really the maximum rate at which anything can move, or is the starship Enterprise's acceleration to 'warp factor 9' a future possibility? This

particular part of our voyage of discovery will include a little technical jargon, although it will be explained in lay-
man's language, so there is nothing to worry about.

We subconsciously (and sometimes consciously) worry
about things we can't explain and try to find rational reasons for them. Unfamiliar happenings make us feel insecure.
Is the 'bump in the night' a dreadful apparition from the
'world beyond', or is it just a door swinging in the wind?
Did I really conjure up that number 47 bus just when the
rain started, or was it only a coincidence? Is there any truth
at all in 'what the stars say', or are these predictions just a
way of selling more newspapers?

We want answers to these questions, not so much
because we want to increase our knowledge but because we
want to feel secure. Anything which is inexplicable or 'different' may possibly be dangerous. There are a few people
who get a genuine thrill from finding the answers to problems; but, for most of us, the reason for finding out about
the Unknown is so that we can sleep more easily at night.
The solutions to the mysteries of the universe you are going
to read about here will satisfy both schools. They will also
open up a whole new way of life for you — if you want
them to — but more of that later.

Before we go any further, it is important to understand
the concept of 'proof'. A lot of new ways of looking at the
universe are going to be described shortly and none of them
can be 'proved'. The answers we find to any of our questions cannot be absolutely 'proved' because nothing can be
definitely and incontrovertibly shown to be 100% true for
now and forever. If you think carefully about proof processes, you will generally find that they are actually no more
than statistical probabilities. Take gravity, for instance. If I let
go of a teacup, it will fall to the ground. Does this 'prove'
that gravity exists? No, it doesn't. It only shows that a peculiarity of space-time which we call gravity existed at the
time the teacup was dropped. But it doesn't prove that grav-

ity exists all of the time. It is true that if gravity didn't exist we would all go flying off into space and, at this moment, we are firmly stuck on planet Earth. But can anyone say with absolute certainty that gravity will still exist in ten minutes' time? There is a high degree of probability that it will, because there is no foreseeable reason why it shouldn't. And any sensible person would happily place a large bet on gravity's continued existence. But lack of a foreseeable reason for something not to happen is not absolute proof that it will happen. We expect and hope that gravity will continue to operate so that teacups will continue to fall and people will stay earth-bound because that is the way our world exists from day to day and we feel 'safe' with the status quo. However, in ten minutes' time, there might be a tiny possibility that we would all go flying off into space because the solar system has, for instance, met a 'naked singularity' (see: *The Edge of Infinity* by Paul Davies, published by J. M. Dent & Sons Ltd,1981) thereby altering our accepted laws of physics. In truth, the 'proof' of the existence of gravity is no more than statistical evidence, gathered from trillions of experiences.

The same can be said for most proofs. They simply represent statistical evidence. 'I'll prove it to you' really means 'I will show you that it will happen'. But there is always a chance in a million that it won't happen. We don't actually know what gravity — or anything else — really is, or why things work in the way that they do, therefore we can only predict the consequences when we let go of a teacup because of previous experiences.

We rely upon statistical probabilities in order to exist in our everyday world. We assume that there is a very high chance that we will normally stay put on the ground and that our teacups won't go drifting off into space. If we didn't accept the predictability of life, we would soon become nervous wrecks. However, in the end, we still have to decide on what we wish to believe and what we wish to disregard;

these choices depend on our emotional security and our *personal* knowledge of the world at the time. So it is up to you whether you decide to believe the things you will be reading about in the following chapters. They cannot be proved, but do they seem *reasonable*? Will they help or hinder you in Life? Will they give you a satisfactory and rational explanation for phenomena such as gravity? Will they give you a clearer reflection of yourself in the pool? Will they delight or frighten you?

The fact that most things which happen in our daily lives are statistically predictable is important because they are the basis of miracles as well as the basis of Mastership. Miracles and magical happenings contradict the everyday rules we accept as the norm. They are events which are not predictable. If someone takes a teacup and causes it to float across the room rather than to crash to the ground, that is magic. The magician has circumvented the law of gravity, and this is not acceptable as a part of our safe, normal, and everyday life. It has not been expected. Unless we can find a logical reason for it we feel uncomfortable and a little insecure. After all, if this unconventional person can levitate teacups, what other things can he do? He becomes a threat unless the levitation can be shown to be a conjuring trick, or he can be revealed to be a 'holy man'. (Holy men, by definition, only do good things and are therefore not regarded as threats). Later on, we will look at the mechanism of miracles and magic and show that there is always a rational explanation for them. They need never be threatening again.

Masters have rid themselves of the terrors of living in an unpredictable world — and the boredom of living in a totally predictable one — by living in the Now. What might happen next week, tomorrow, or in the next minute is not important to them: awareness of the Now is all that really matters. They have reached a level of absolute trust in the events of the world: for them, whatever happens is the right thing to happen and therefore it can never be threatening or 'bad'. This doesn't mean that they don't plan ahead. They still arrange to go on trips; decide on what they are going to have for dinner and go to the shops for the ingredients; and launder their clothes so that they will have clean ones to put on the next day just like everyone else. But if their plans go awry, it doesn't matter to them; it really doesn't matter at all. They are not put out when circumstances change; they always 'keep their cool'.

Put another way, they have solved the riddle of time. Although this book is not a shortcut to Mastership, it may help to demonstrate that time is nothing like what we generally accept it to be. Rather it has aspects which can be used to show us quicker ways along the path. Conversely, another aspect of this journey we will discover more about is that, in the end, speed in itself is not important: it is only our awareness that matters. Getting to the goal is less important than being aware of and enjoying the delights we meet along the way. A lot of this book is given over to glimpses of the captivating radiance of our universe.

Another important aspect of life, which many of us prefer not to face, is the need to take chances. One of the greatest paradoxes of human existence is that we automatically seek security whenever we can, and yet we can only make progress by putting ourselves into unfamiliar situations. Day-to-day plans keep us ticking over; but progress along our particular life-path is achieved only by taking chances in situations where we have to have a measure of trust. The very act of walking is a continuous process of moving from balance to unbalance and back to balance again. It is not possible for a biped to move forward unaided and at a reasonable speed without taking a foot off the ground and leaning first a little bit backwards and then forwards. These actions automatically move the walker in and out of balance. Try walking consciously and you will see what I mean. We are so used to walking that we have automatic trust in the process. Masters have this sort of trust in all that they do and all that happens to them.

It is all too easy to sink comfortably into the state where we know with a fair degree of certainty what is going to happen to us each day and thereby feel secure. But, if we were to take an honest look at ourselves, we would find that there is deep down an underlying sense of dissatisfaction with this wholly predictable state of affairs. Life eventually becomes soporific and boring. We need challenges to give zest and purpose to existence. Prehistoric man found plenty of challenges in just foraging for food to keep himself and his family alive. But as more and more inventions came along to make life easier, the number of challenges diminished almost to the point of extinction. Today, most of us need to invent challenges or else experience them vicariously by watching sport or other peoples' endeavours on television. But there are actually plenty of worthwhile challenges left; and one of the greatest of all is our individual journey back to 'God'.

The word 'God' is in inverted commas because it means something completely different to different people. The sort of 'God' to be considered here is not the common idea of a father-figure, or someone to be worshiped. In fact, it is not a religious figurehead at all; rather, it is based on the innate feeling that there is more to life than simply keeping the physical body alive. Most people feel that there is a 'something' or 'someone' hidden away somewhere who has our welfare at heart and takes ultimately responsibility for us. They consider this to be the same super-being who created our universe and should therefore be worshiped as the source of all things. To some, 'He' is judgmental and will punish wrongdoers; to others 'He' is merciful and will 'forgive us our trespasses'; meanwhile some reckon that a word in 'His' ear will ensure success in hazardous projects such as battles or take-over bids. All these attributes are, unfortunately, very human and based on fear or wishful thinking — they are part of our need for security as I mentioned earlier.

But the ultimate 'God' to which our inward/outward journey is taking us is not a personality at all; so being judgmental, merciful, vengeful, or partial, along with any other human traits, cannot be part of 'His' image. Therefore, in order to move us away from well-worn religious tracks, we will rename the final destination of our journey, 'Cosmos'.

The idea of Cosmos is more akin to Buddhist or Taoist philosophies than western ones. Neither of these two religions has a Super-being in charge. Buddhism sets the responsibility for the behaviour of its followers squarely on their own shoulders. To reach their particular paradise, Nirvana, they need to abide by a set of precepts. If they don't fulfil all the requirements, they come back life after life until a proper balance has been achieved. (See the chapter on Reincarnation). God doesn't reward or punish them; the Law of Karma does. (See the chapter on Karma).

Taoist philosophy requires its followers to return to, or remain in, a state of innocence — not virginal innocence, or mental ignorance, but in a state where all happenings are accepted without question. This is the way back to Tao. The word 'Tao' is indefinable. In fact, the very beginning of the Tao Te Ching, which is the main book of Taoism, says that 'The Tao that can be expressed is not the Unchanging Tao: the Name that can be named is not the Unchanging Name'. Nevertheless, rough translations of Tao are 'The Way', 'Truth', or 'The Source'.

So, Cosmos is nearer to Tao than anything else because it is the Source of all things — *all* things. And this is the 'place', 'thing', or whatever you want to call it, which we are trying to reach. 'No, I'm not,' you say, 'I'm just trying to scrape an honest living and live in peace.' And that is your honest opinion at this moment. But . . . . you will find as you read on that you have forgotten many of your original objectives in life. Part of the purpose of this book is to remind you of what you once promised yourself always to remember at those times when you were more aware of your soul, that you are a tiger rather than a goat.

In the end, when we have looked at our divine tigerness in the pool, and when we have solved the mysteries and become conversant with miracles, we will once again remember that our ultimate objective remains as it always was — to return to the Source, to Cosmos. That is our eternal journey, and we are all travelling it in different ways. During the course of this book, we will see what makes the journey easier, what forms barriers, and how to find pools. We will also discover techniques to make the process of the journey more enjoyable. All in all, the journey is one of discovery about Life, Godliness and Ourselves. And, most important of all, it is a journey full of delights to be experienced along the way.

Chapter 2

Don't Forget the Stars

We now know that we are going on our journey primarily to re-discover our divine tigerness. We know where we are going — back to the Source — and we know what to do while we are travelling — that is, to re-discover our delight in living, to stay aware, and to enjoy the scenery. What we now need to find out is what sort of terrain we will be travelling through and if there is any special equipment we should take. The next few chapters will discuss these topics. They will describe in particular some of the fascinating oddities of time, space and energy. These are three of the most influential phenomena we live with; thus an understanding of what they really are is important, so that they might enhance our enjoyment of the journey and help us in our daily lives.

As we live in time and space, and use energy in order to exist, we are all familiar with the everyday workings of these things . . . . Or so we think . . . . Time and space are so much part of our surroundings that we generally don't notice that they exist. We are rather like fish swimming in water: they have no idea of what water is; they simply accept that they can move about by flapping their fins. Similarly, we accept that we live in a system where tomorrow follows today, and the next town is a distance away. However, while such acceptance is reasonable in our daily routines, a deeper knowledge is needed if we are to become truly aware of the finer details of our universe and the meaning of such mysteries as 'spirit', 'soul', the 'Real Self' and Cosmos.

So let's start by looking at the phenomenon we call 'space'. Our bodies exist in space and the feeling we have about it is that it is a Very Useful Thing because it separates us from others and gives us room to move around without coming too close to other beings. We generally see space in this way — as a separator. When feeling particularly vulnerable, people say, 'Don't crowd me; I need my space.' This is all very well, but all things, apart from Cosmos, have opposites, so space is also a connector. It is what physically unites us with each other. Just as a telephone exchange not only connects two parties, but also separate them from all other subscribers, so space both connects and separates things within it. The connecting aspect of space is very important to our Journey.

Francis Thompson, a poet who lived at the end of the 19th century put this very aptly in his poem 'The Mistress of Vision':

> *When to the new eyes of thee*
> *All things by immortal power,*
> *Near or far,*
> *Hiddenly*
> *To each other linkèd are,*
> *That thou canst not stir a flower*
> *Without troubling of a star.*

Or, to put it more simply, everything anyone does affects everyone and everything else sooner or later. When I pick a flower, I affect what will happen on the star Betelgeuse, albeit minutely. Francis Thompson is saying that all things are interconnected and interdependent. *All* things. There are no exceptions. Flowers, stars, mountains, mole-hills, people, animals, electrons, germs multiplying in the sewers, satellites spinning round the world: they are all interconnected and interdependent. I, the writer, am connected to you by this book. I have written what you are reading. It will go into your memory and may affect your outlook on life. Thus we are connected by my action in writing and your action in reading. Buying the book will have affected your financial situation; or borrowing it from the library will have affected your total energy level as you lifted it off the shelf. Writing the book on a computer affected the total electrical energy supply of the British Isles. Sending the manuscript to a publisher affected the lives of postal workers, proof-readers, editors, typesetters, and others. None of these effects were very large; nevertheless they did occur. And sometimes what appear at first to be very small effects can turn out to have startlingly large consequences . . . .

Just as an exercise, imagine the dictator of some unspecified country getting up in the morning, still undecided on the fate of his latest political rival. At breakfast, he asks for his favourite jam, and is told that there is none left. (The chef had forgotten to re-order the jam, because he had been worrying about his daughter's outrageous hair-style. She had had her hair coloured in red and green stripes to shock one of her school friends because he had called her a 'square'. He had called her a square because he had been angry with his mother and had had to take his anger out on someone dear to him, etc.)

So the jam-less dictator is in a bad mood and makes the decision to execute his rival. The execution leads to a mass uprising of the people, and a great and bloody battle in which the dictator is overthrown. So, following the logical sequence, the overthrow of the dictator can be attributed to the chef's forgetfulness; which can be traced back to the frustrations and reactions of his spirited daughter, her boyfriend and her boyfriend's mother; which, in turn, might have been responses to a remark by a shoe-shine boy about the weather or by a passing glance of a taxi driver at a pretty girl. Thus, there is the possibility that a casual remark or the lilt of a girl's walk can overthrow a government. So, by simple deduction, we can say that all human activities follow similar patterns and can be traced back to apparently trivial origins.

We seldom recognise these trivialities, except in retro-spect. We can be fairly sure that Newton didn't say to his wife: 'I'll just go out to the orchard and invent the theory of gravity.' No, he more likely said: 'I feel like a breath of air after that excellent lunch, dear, so I'll go and sit in the orchard for a bit.' If Mrs Newton hadn't been given a side of venison by her neighbour and turned it into a wonderful lunch, would we still be wondering why things fall when we let go of them? Unlikely; but possible. That joint of veni-son may be responsible for space travel (and non-stick saucepans which are a spin-off from research into new space-age materials).

Continuing along the gravitational track, we all know about the effects of gravity and Newton's third law of motion — action and reaction are equal and opposite — so we know that theoretically, when you jump into the air, not only do you move away from the earth, but the earth also moves away from you. So your jump must also move all the people and things on this planet by a very, very small amount. This is a physical fact. The amount of the move-ment is so tiny that there probably isn't a fraction of a micro-millimetre small enough to express it. Nevertheless, the the-ory of modern physics would break down if Newton's basic laws were not true for all normal physical things throughout the universe. Thus, your action in moving away from the earth when you jump, must create an equal reaction in the earth, causing it to move away from you. And the move-ment of every other thing in the world is causing reactive movement in everything else too. So, physically we are all interconnected in the how, where and when of motion when we move. We are also obviously interconnected in the air we breathe, the water we use, the materials we recycle, and so on. The amounts of interconnectedness are minute but they definitely do exist. And the interconnectedness does not apply solely to things existing *now*. The water we drink once held neolithic swimmers, and some of their skin follicles washed off. Those follicles still exist in the water, and they may have attached themselves to our skin. Each one of us carries around the debris of the living and the dead dating from the ~~the~~ dawn of the universe. *The very molecules from which we are made were once parts of stars in distant galaxies.* We are truly made from star-dust.

But while it is important to recognise these physical connections, they are not the ones that Francis Thompson is primarily talking about; and they are not the only ones we are going to look at in this book. As the tale of the dictator's downfall illustrated, we are connected to each other emotionally, mentally, and physically. We are also connected spiritually, as any religion will tell you. All these interconnections are aspects of a universal phenomenon which, for want of a better title, will be called the Lattice of Life.

This Lattice is not a hypothetical device invented to serve as an example of cosmic connectedness. It actually exists. Put very simply, the Lattice is a non-physical multi-dimensional lattice of strands of cosmic 'stuff' which interconnects all aspects of the universe at its various levels. It fills the universe in all directions, and there is no part of existence which is not connected by it. We cannot see, hear, smell, taste, or touch it because it is non-physical; but it is all around us, through us and a part of us throughout time. It connects the flowers I touch on our planet, Earth, with the distant star Betelgeuse, and all the other heavenly bodies. It connects the ideas you are now reading on this page with the day-dreams of draft oxen in India, and the complex mathematical calculations of a professor at the Massachusetts Institute of Technology. It connects the thoughts, feelings, and emotions of all six billion people on this planet to each other and to life-forms on the furthermost parts of the Milky Way. It was here before the universe was created, and it will be here after the universe ends. Over the centuries, it has been acknowledged by some philosophers and ridiculed by others. H P Blavatsky writes about it in

The Secret Doctrine where she calls it *The Web of the Universe* and says that it connects Spirit with Matter.

There is no way, ultimately, to prove its existence; and there is no way, ultimately, to disprove it either. (Remember the discussion about 'proofs' in chapter 1). It is non-physical, so there are no instruments available with which to measure it, and our normal five senses cannot recognise it. Nevertheless, it connects us to all things at all levels: physically, emotionally, mentally and spiritually. It is also an important agent in our link with Cosmos.

The Lattice is an important concept in our Journey, so we will examine it in the next chapter from a variety of vantage points in order to establish its status as a reasonable hypothesis. If no major objections can be found, we will be able to use it to explain some of the strange occurrences in the universe, thereby discovering more about our environment and ourselves. But, as is the case with all the descriptions and explanations in this book, the final decision as to its acceptance and usage is left to each one of us.

Chapter 3

Universal Lifelines

If the statement in the last chapter is true, and the Lattice existed even before the universe came into being, we need to look at the possible interactions between these two important phenomena. Did the universe appear as a result of some peculiarity of the Lattice? Are they independent or interdependent? Where does Cosmos, (God), fit or not fit into the overall picture? Is the Lattice just a metaphysical concept or can it have a scientific basis? If the statement is not true, then our investigation will make this obvious, and the preceding questions will have no answers.

This question concerning scientific bases is very important with respect to the widespread acceptance of the Lattice existence. Many metaphysical ideas are rejected by conventional scientists because they are 'unscientific', that is they do not stand up to laboratory investigation or they go against accepted scientific principles. Any theory concerning the basic structure of the universe should be reasonable from both the points of view of the scientific establishment as well as that of people who see things from a spiritual standpoint. This is one of the difficulties with many of the ideas put forward by both schools. A large number of scientific systems have no room for anything which is associated with the spiritual or metaphysics; and a lot of spiritual theses ignore the scientific questions which they raise.

Consider the large number of scientists who have been hounded by their colleagues for daring to question established thinking: eminent people such as Galileo; Helmholtz; Gauss; Faraday; Pauli. And then consider the number of people who feel that they know better than incontrovertible scientific facts, such as the Flat Earth Society, Alice Bailey's belief in the planet Vulcan, and all the people who reckon that they have ridden in flying saucers and conversed with 'little green men'. On the one hand, we find the unshakable dogmatism of blinkered scientists and on the other, we find the gullibility of wishful thinkers. We need to steer a clear path between these extremes, and look at the structure and operation of the Lattice as dispassionately as possible. The detailed doctrines concerning both science and spirit are too obscure for this type of book, but the general theories on which they are based can be explained quite simply. In the process we won't get involved in complex mathematics or profound doctrinal arguments.

To begin at the Beginning of All Things, there are three main scientific theories about the creation of the universe. The most popular one at present is the Big Bang theory — that the whole universe was created by the explosion of a very small but infinitely dense piece of matter, which contained all the constituents that now form the universe. The second theory, Continuous Creation, says that there was no one single act of creation at all — the universe keeps on creating new matter all the time. It always has and it always will. The third one is based more on religion than on science. It states that the universe had no beginning and will have no end. It keeps cyclically expanding and contracting, like the process of breathing.

There is no means of proving any of these theories. Additionally, the Big Bang theory raises the subsidiary question of where the original lump of dense matter came from, but ultimately the decision as to which is right has to be based on opinions. (I like this one more than that; my instincts tell me that this one is true; my religion tells me that that one is the Truth). Two thousand years ago the theories were different, and two thousand years from now they will be different yet again. Just at the moment, the majority of influential thinkers favour the Big Bang, but another theory will probably be in vogue fifty years from now.

If we look dispassionately at the views of both the scientific and religious establishment orthodoxies, we will see that most new ideas, when first presented, are accepted or rejected as a result of the opinions of influential thinkers rather than for their proof processes. (Consider the present arguments raging in scientific circles concerning Fleischmann's nuclear 'cold fusion' process, and the recent furore in religious circles concerning the authenticity of the Turin shroud). It is helpful to remember that however mighty the establishment, it is still run by human beings with their human frailties. The greatest minds on earth are still vulnerable to prejudice, emotions and the availability of jam for breakfast. Therefore there is the possibility that any, or all of them, can make the occasional error.

As far as religion is concerned, the Creation has always been a magical event. Religion and mythology overlap in giving super-beings the credit for creating the universe out of a great variety of things ranging from Light (Judaism and Christianity), Breath (Hinduism), to Chaos (the Pelasgians), and various extraordinary animals (myths). All these stories are allegorical and were invented as simple explanations to satisfy mankind's insatiable curiosity. For thousands of years, families have entertained themselves telling stories round the fireside, and most of the myths are a result of those fireside sessions. They were modified and spread from culture to culture by the professional story tellers of earlier times, so that we now find the same basic story with local embellishments occurring in widely separated parts of the world. We will see later that the workings of the Lattice are fully compatible with the creation myths, and are able to give them deeper meaning. Just for the moment, let us accept the reasonable hypothesis that there *was* some sort of process of creation for the universe, and look at the implications of this.

Imagine you are observing the vastness of space *before* the universe was formed: before the infinitely dense piece of matter exploded into existence; before Eurynome rose naked from Chaos; before God said 'Let there be Light'. It is an infinite nothingness stretching in all directions. There is nothing in it; it is absolutely black and empty. (There are no stars or suns, so no light can be generated). This is the inky blackness of pre-creation. *But the space is not actually empty* — it is full of the myriad strings forming the structure of the Lattice. These strings are non-physical. They cannot be seen, touched or measured. They are not composed of matter, gravity or electromagnetic waves; they do not exist in 'time' because time has not been formulated yet. This is the period of pre-creation, so let's call it non-time, and let the lightless blackness be non-space. The strings can be imagined as pathways. They are the non-time, non-space 'grooves' in which life will eventually run. They are not composed of the matter of life itself; they are the future 'lines of communication' from one pattern of life to the next. In the same way that telephone lines carry speech but are not the speech itself, so the Lattice strings simply act as *carriers* for matter, energy, thoughts, feelings and all the other paraphernalia of the phenomenon which we call life.

So far as the basic Lattice is concerned, it doesn't matter whether the universe was created by a Big Bang, the continuous creation of new matter, or a super-being. Whatever the form of Creation, the Lattice was already there, waiting for the contents of the universe to be hung upon it. As it says in Blavatsky's Secret Doctrine, 'Father-Mother spin a Web . . . . this is the Web of the Universe' (*Stanzas of Dzyan III*).

Scientific writers in the 19th century referred to the stuff of non-space as 'the aether' and believed that it acted as a carrier of electromagnetism. The big difference between their supposition and the one being presented to you now is that the aether was supposed to be a sort of non-material all-pervading gas; whereas the Lattice is composed of non-material distinct and separate strings. These strings stretch past infinity in all directions and there is *nothing* between them: no gas; no electromagnetic fields; no physical presence of any sort.

This difference, this nothingness between the strings, is vitally important. Without the 'nothingness gaps' modern scientific ideas such as quantum theory cannot be properly accounted for; and to satisfy both the scientific and spiritual establishments, the Lattice *must* be able to support both views. By accepting that the gaps exist, both quantum theory and relativity are explainable, as are spiritual and paranormal phenomena such as miracles, magic and God (Cosmos).

Before we go on and look in more detail at the construction of the Lattice itself, we had better dispose of the question concerning the Lattice origin, because it has no answer. Unanswerable questions are a normal part of life, and they need to be acknowledged; otherwise, they leave nagging doubts. If there *were* an answer to the origin of the Lattice it would only lead to the next question concerning the origin of the thing before the Lattice, and so on. It is as pointless as debating the length of a piece of string or the starting point of a circle. All series of questions beginning with 'why' or 'where' can go on for ever because there is no such thing as an ultimate reason or an ultimate place. The Lattice origin will be dealt with satisfactorily in the next chapter when we come to consider the structure of time. For the moment, please accept, with as many reservations as you like, that the Lattice came from nowhere and has always existed.

So let's look at the form of the Lattice itself. It is composed of 'non-material' and has no real form, but in order to get some idea of how it works, we need to visualise it as a simple structure. Although it is multi-dimensional, in order to build up an image of how it works, consider it first as a two-dimensional lattice-work (see Figure 1). The strings — which have no thickness) — are separated by gaps. These strings simply act as communication lines for the energies of life which flow through the Lattice. The energies contain all possible forms of life existing in the universe: animal; veg-

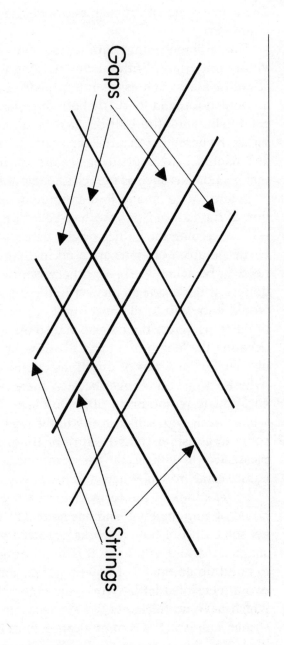

Figure 1. Two dimensional Lattice structure

etable; mineral; emotional; mental; visionary; intuitional; spiritual; etc.

The gaps do not contain anything. This doesn't mean that there is a vacuum between the strings; it means that there is *no existence at all* between the strings. It is as if the gaps were in another universe — like the parallel universe concept beloved of science fiction writers. Anything able to shift into the gaps would totally disappear from this universe. Although this is a difficult idea to accept, it makes the peculiar antics of some sub-atomic particles easier to believe. (Such as the fact that some of these special particles — muons, leptrons, etc. — seem able to jump instantaneously from one place to another at speeds far exceeding the relativistic limiting speed of light). It also touches on the latest scientific theories concerning 'wormholes in space' which allow matter to move instantaneously from one part of the universe to another. As far as the Lattice theory is concerned, existence, as we know it, only occurs *along the strings of the Lattice*. Existence in this universe is impossible between the strings; and all observable phenomena in the universe are seen as vibrational patterns caused by movements of life energy along the strings themselves. These patterns are observed as everything we know about from, say, the movement of electrons round an atomic nucleus to the majesty of the Andes mountains.

The crossover points of the strings are where energy is concentrated, and these form the pinpoints of power which go to constitute the solid shapes we see. Just like the pictures we see in the newspaper are actually composed of thousands of dots, so the solids we see all around us are actually composed of millions of atoms and those atoms are in turn composed of millions of energy points (see Figure 2).

There are so many strings in the Lattice, and they are so close together, that it is impossible to see the actual crossover points, even with the most powerful scientific microscope. We assume that the shapes they form are con-

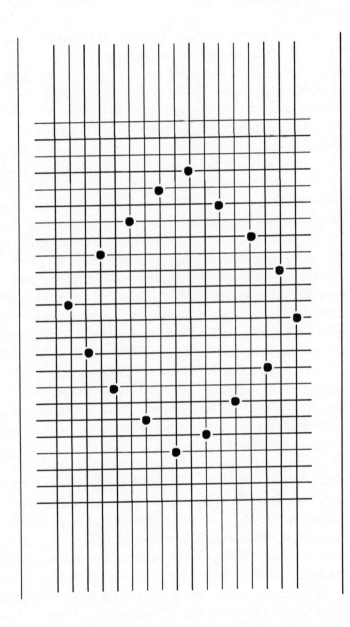

Figure 2. Pattern made by Lattice crossovers

tinuous — just like we assume a chair is continuous even though we know that it is actually composed of trillions of atoms with large gaps in between. Note that the vibrating energy in each string only forms one power point, or 'node', with the energy of one other string; that is, energy lines only interact with one other line at a time.

The full picture of the Lattice is far broader than the two-dimensional representation shown in figure 2. It is multi-dimensional, with strings going off in all directions: that is with strings going in and out of the paper as well as up and down and left and right. The strings are always separated by gaps and these gaps are very important. If all the points of the Lattice are separated by gaps it is reasonable to assume that all the matter in the universe is also discontinuous. We already accept this at an atomic level, (consider the example of the chair given previously); but the Lattice theory takes this one stage further and says that the energies within *each sub-atomic particle* are likewise discontinuous. There are no ultimate 'solids' in the universe. All things ultimately reduce to patterns of points of energy. Some physicists talk about space having a 'foam-like' structure at these levels way below the atomic. (See *The Edge of Infinity* by Paul Davies, page 179). This 'foamy space' concept is closely in line with the Lattice theory.

There are also physicists who think that time as well as space is discontinuous. They have called the shortest possible interval of time a 'jiffy' and theorise that it was the first jump into reality that occurred at the commencement of the Big Bang. It has been calculated as about a three million billion billion billionth (3×10^{-42}) of a second, using the British type of billion i.e. one million times one million. This is such a minuscule number that it is quite impossible to imagine; and it is therefore no wonder that we see time as a continuous function. Even using the power of the most modern apparatus, the shortest time measurable is in the region of one thousandth of a billion billionth (10^{-27}) of a second, which is still about three thousand billion times (3×10^{15}) too large.

Thus it is possible that existence as we know it consists of a series of short flashes of time interspersed with periods of non-existence in a universe which is made up of lots of individual nodules of matter scattered on a fabric of non-space. This is the structure of the Lattice. It cannot be proved to exist because its structure is non-material and non-temporal. Therefore it is beyond logical understanding because logic only works as a continuous process. Science is generally logical until it gets down to sub-atomic levels and the idiosyncrasies of quantum theory. Down amongst the muons and quarks of this universe, all sorts of peculiar and illogical things happen. Particles can be in two places at once; they can also 'communicate' with each other, and seem able to foretell the future. New theories are being expounded all the time in order to account for these inconsistencies, but they only seem to lead to more problems.

On the other hand, spirituality has always relied on illogical happenings in order to exist . . . . miracles, omnipotent and omniscient beings, voices from burning bushes, etc. The Lattice has the ability to integrate the observations of science and the convictions of the spiritual without compromise. Science will still be able to celebrate a logical universe; and the spiritual will still be able to revere divine beings and magical happenings.

Familiarity with these diverse teachings is an integral part of our journey. This does not mean that the traveller needs to be fully conversant with the esoteric details of either discipline, but a passing knowledge certainly enriches the adventure. Like any other pleasurable walk, a simple understanding of the flora and fauna helps to enhance one's enjoyment. It is also true that 'knowledge' does not imply blind acceptance. Gullibility is as far from the path as is bigotry.

In the next chapter, we will look at the peculiarities of non-space and non-time in more detail. They are the key to an understanding of Cosmos itself. As Cosmos is the custodian of the Source, the next few pages are vital to our full understanding of the purpose of our exploration.

Chapter 4

Now You See It . . . .
Now you Don't

In the last chapter, the Lattice was described as being non-material and non-temporal, that is to say not part of space and time as we know them. This 'non-ness' is a difficult concept to grasp because everything we normally deal with is a part of these two familiar quantities which give us space in which to move and time in which to think. We cannot imagine anything which is not basically a combination of the two. Therefore all descriptions of the true structure of the Lattice will fall short of its actual reality. In these circumstances, what we have to do is use similes to get us a part of the way towards the truth, and then leave intuition to do the rest. In order to fully exploit the similes, we will also be looking at one or two basic principles concerning both atoms and energy in order to satisfy both scientific and the spiritual establishments. These scientific ideas are explained in very simple terms, so get comfortable; take the phone off the hook, and read on. . . .

First of all, let's look at the gaps between the Lattice strings. These gaps are actually more important than the strings themselves because they contain the *origin of all that ever was, or is, or will be*. The strings are the pathways that support life; but the gaps are either where Cosmos (God) resides, (if you see things from a spiritual point of view), or where the potential energy of the universe is held, (if you see things from a scientific point of view). Both of these concepts — Cosmos and potential energy — come out of the nothingness in the gaps, and all the 'stuff' of the universe then comes from one or the other notion. Most of this chapter will be spent in showing how it is not only possible but also reasonable for *all* our somethings to come from the idea of nothingness. As far as our logical minds are concerned, nothingness is the only place, or non-place, where non-space and non-time can possibly be.

You may think that you already understand the concept of nothingness. 'Nothing means the absence of something', you say, or words to that effect. But the reality of nothingness is not as simple as that, as we shall shortly discover. In fact, it has been paradoxically stated many times by many sages that anyone who *really* understands the significance of 'nothing' automatically understands all there is to know about everything. It is unlikely that we shall reach that sublime state in this chapter, (or even in this book) but, as the sages also delight in saying, 'A journey of a thousand miles starts with a single step'. So off we go on that first step. . . .

One of the ways of deciding whether a concept is true or not is to assume that it *is* true and then to test that truth by fitting everyday situations into it. If they fit, the concept may well be true: if any of the situations doesn't fit, then the concept must be false. So let us start from the statement: *'Everything comes out of nothing.'* This is a simple statement which embraces the whole of existence. It may be true: it may not. Let's examine it in more detail to find out. Everything comes out of nothing. What does it mean? At face value it seems to be an impossibility. How can something come out of nothing? But if you think about it just a little bit more, it can be shown to be based on reality. As an example: a book can be reduced to pages: pages can be reduced to paper: paper can be reduced to a composition of vegetable pulps, pulps to chemical constituents, and so on down to molecules, atoms, electrons, neutrons, quarks . . . . until eventually we are left with nothing but elusive energy fields and vague areas of probability. The game of particle physics goes on and on, discovering — or inventing? — smaller and smaller and more and more obscure particles and energy fields to account for the growing number of paradoxes which occur in this sub-atomic wonderland. To date, physicists have a list of about 200 sub-atomic particles, including a number of anti-mass particles which, so far as we know, can only have existence in mathematical equations. The list is still growing as both theoretical and practical anomalies are counteracted by yet more ingenious discoveries. Thus, the pages of this book and all other things that we take for granted as solid and real are actually derived from vague and unpredictable energy fields. Our 'somethings' seem to start out from a hotchpotch of 'nothings'.

It doesn't matter whether we are considering the pages of this book, the mountains on the moon, or someone's little finger nail; the same process of finding that the apparently solid matter is actually vague nothings still applies. So the statement that 'everything comes out of nothing' seems to be reasonable. It makes no difference to our daily life. We still expect a chair to support our weight when we sit down, and don't expect to fall through the gaps between the molecules, electron fields, and so on. However, this idea of nothing being the source of all things will be a great help in our journey towards a better understanding of Self and Cosmos.

Now let's look a little more closely at the concept of 'existence'. After all, our general idea of existence is the presence of something within space and time. However, if these phenomena are suspect, then maybe existence is suspect too.

According to modern scientific thinking, the existence of a great many of the atomic particles we know and love is clouded with uncertainty. Some of the energies from which even such particles as the ubiquitous electron are derived are said to have existed for only a brief snippet of time at the very start of the universe. Others have never been isolated or measured, but are necessary to make energy equations balance. Most of them are subject to Heisenberg's Uncertainty Principle, which is one of the corner stones of modern atomic theory. This principle says that if the position of a particle is known, then we don't know for sure what that particle is doing, and if we know what it is doing we can't be sure where it is. We can't be sure of both place and activity at the same time; one or the other has to be uncertain. Therefore, these particles cannot be precisely defined.

The startling result of this principle is that the movements of particles are reduced to statistical probabilities. We can only talk about their activities in 'chance' terms. For example, if we bombard a specific particle with other particles, the chances are that it will either move off in a given direction, or maybe break down into a selection of yet more types of particle. Until the action takes place we can't be certain of the result. But *statistically* we know the result which will be achieved on a large-scale basis involving lots and lots of particles. It's a bit like trying to predict the behaviour of a football crowd. An observer cannot say for certain what an individual member of the crowd will do at the end of the match, but the overall movement of the crowd will certainly be towards the exit gates.

So we can see that even the high technology which we have come to accept as precise and totally logical actually contains large areas of doubt. Our modern sciences can safely land a space-craft on the moon and design computers of enormous complexity, but they are by no means perfect. Certain things have yet to be discovered and the more the physicists delve into the small details of existence, the more difficult it becomes to keep pure logic as a basic analytical tool. Even the descriptions of certain sub-atomic particles such as quarks now include attributes such as 'strangeness' and 'charm'. Precise mathematical language is no longer adequate to describe the wonderland of quantum physics. However, by using the ideas on which the Lattice is based, it is possible for us to take another step forward into this strange and fascinating area, starting with concepts concerning zero. Once zero is understood, we have more of a chance in understanding about the things which emerge from zero — the things that make up our universe.

The number from which all other numbers are produced — the 'starting point' — is Zero, or Nothing. It is the beginning of most numerical series: 0, 1, 2, 3, 4, ..., or 0, 1, 2, 4, 8, 16, ... And Nothing is also the point from which *something* is produced. Noise comes out of silence; light comes out of darkness, and so on. 'Nothing' seems to be a big box full of everything we need; but we can't look into the box; we can only make things appear from it as if by magic.

Have you ever consciously tried to imagine 'no-thing'? It is impossible. However hard you try to visualise nothing, something will always appear on the scene. If you imagine a hole getting bigger and bigger, it will always have an edge. If you imagine the emptiness of space, there will always be comets, planets, or dust getting in the way. If you imagine the symbol 0, it is only the representation of the non-quantity you are trying to focus on. However hard you try, there will always be an existence of some sort to spoil the non-existence of nothingness. Ultimately, the very fact that *you* are there, imagining the nothing, destroys its nothingness. The ability to cease to exist when contemplating nothingness is the pinnacle of spiritual achievement desired by every true disciple seeking ultimate Truth.

Just as an exercise, and to reinforce the concept that total annihilation of existence is impossible, let us try very hard, and with no expense spared, to create just a little piece of nothingness. By nothingness, we mean a completely non-observable, non-measurable, non-reacting state of existence. Start with an empty box, say of about the size of a matchbox, and connect it to a vacuum pump to extract all the gases from it. Let us suppose that the pump is extraordinarily efficient and can actually pull the very last molecule of gas out of the box. Have we got nothing in the box now? Unfortunately not; all sorts of radiation are still present within: radioactive waves; radio waves; telepathic waves; (if you 'believe' in them); gravity waves; and so on. So, we will make the box out of lead to prohibit entry of the radioactive and radio waves, and find some special material which will also stop all telepathic-type waves. To remove the gravity waves, we will take it out to some remote part of the galaxy where there are no gravitational forces from nearby planets or stars.

Surely our box will be full of nothing now? Unfortunately not because the materials of the box itself contain mass, and mass creates gravity, so the very fact that the box exists at all means that it cannot contain nothing! The only way to produce a box full of nothing would be to make it of a massless material able to stop all forms of radiation. Maybe such a non-material exists somewhere in the universe, but as far as present-day technology is concerned, we must accept that it is impossible to have even a matchboxful of nothing. Alternatively, 'nothing' could be produced by increasing the size of the box until it was larger than the universe. It would actually need to be a great deal larger for the mass of the material of its walls to cease to have any gravitational effect. As this is obviously impossible, the production of nothingness must also be acknowledged to be an impossibility.

Note that the previous sentence referred to the 'production' of nothingness; that is, it is not possible for any of the 'somethings' which already exist in the universe to be reduced to nothing. But the Lattice is full of nothingness: the gaps contain only nothingness and it has always been there. Right from before time began. Here is the dilemma: all the 'stuff' of the universe actually exists as flows of energy forming patterns of matter interspersed with areas of nothingness. But, though this nothingness is an integral part of all of existence, we cannot make *physical* contact with it.

To understand why this is so, we need first of all to look at and understand what 'potential' really means. Don't get worried — this will not turn into a lecture on abstruse

physics or mathematics, and all these explanations will
eventually make the object of our existence — our journey
— easier to understand. These concepts about energy and
how it works are absolutely basic to a comprehension of the
workings of the universe and especially of the Lattice. They
may also prove to be useful in our daily lives. Although the
words 'potential' and 'dynamic' are going to be especially
associated with energy in the following description, they can
well be equally applied to almost any aspect of life.

First of all — what do we mean by energy? Energy can be
defined in scientific terms as 'the capacity to do work'. In
everyday language it is the ability to act, to move, to produce power, to be alive. Note that it does not have to be
action itself, or an actual movement, but only the *ability to
act or move*. If a thing is without energy, it cannot move, act,
or work. In fact, it cannot exist at all. All things in existence
contain energy in some form or another. *If it were possible for
them to lose all their energy, they would vanish, and cease to exist.*
They would become nothing, and we now know that this is
impossible. It is also a basic law of physics that energy cannot be destroyed; it can only be changed into other forms of
energy or matter. Even at a temperature of absolute zero,
(which is the lowest possible temperature of anything in the
universe), particles of matter are still moving about and contain energy. Science tells us that anything at a temperature of
absolute zero has reached its minimum possible energy
state, but even at this level it still exists. It still has *being*. In
general terms, *energy is synonymous with being, or life*. 'Death'
in this context simply implies a change of existence from one
form of life to another.

If something has potential energy it means that the thing
is capable of *doing* something, but has not yet started doing
it. It is in a 'waiting' state. It is not yet active, or 'dynamic'.
Potential energy is energy which is there to be worked with
but which is not yet being used. It is stored energy. 'He is a
potential trouble-maker' means that he *could* be a nuisance

but is not one yet. 'This is a potentially lethal situation' implies that death is a possible outcome but things have not yet degenerated that far. The *quality* of 'potential energy' is an inactivity which may, or may not, manifest itself as action at some time in the future. 'To be or not to be' is the state of potentialism.

On the other hand, if something is dynamic it means that it is *actively engaged in doing something*. It is not 'waiting' but 'doing'. Dynamic energy is energy which is working *now*. It is active energy. It comes from the Greek word 'dynamism' meaning 'power', while potential comes from the Latin word 'potens' meaning 'to be able'. *These are the only two basic types of energy possible.* All the energy in the universe is either dynamic or potential, and all things in the universe contain a combination of these two energy states.

Thus everything and everyone in the universe is actively engaged in 'doing' and partly occupied with 'waiting'. This is an important realisation — that everyone and everything has potential to be something else and to do other things. Ores are waiting to become metals; seeds are waiting to become plants; oceans are waiting to become rain; goats are waiting to become tigers; and we are waiting to complete our journey and become enlightened. Whether we actually make full use of the potential we have within us depends upon a lot of factors, but the point to give great considera-tion to at this stage is that, whoever we are and whatever we are doing, there is an energy inside us waiting to help us to do a lot more.

To have a clear understanding of this important differ-ence between dynamic and potential energies, consider the movement of a clock's pendulum. When the clock is first made, the clockmaker moves the pendulum to one end of its travel, ready to let it go and see if the clock will operate properly. At this moment the pendulum has potential ener-gy, but no dynamic energy. It has the capacity for movement (potential energy), because it would swing across in an arc

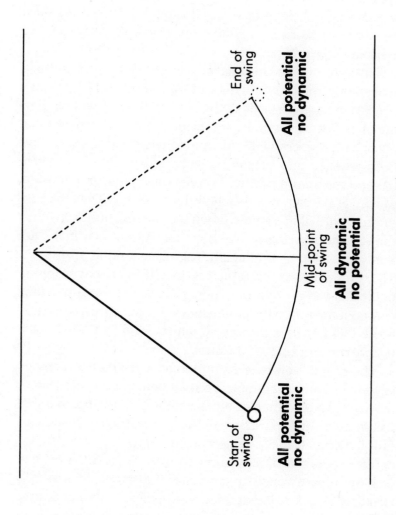

Start of swing
All potential no dynamic

Mid-point of swing
All dynamic no potential

End of swing
All potential no dynamic

Figure 3. The pendulum

to the other end of its travel if the clockmaker removes his fingers . But while he holds on to it, it does not move, and so it has no dynamic energy. It would remain in this motionless state for ever if the clockmaker either holds on to it, or ties it in place with a piece of string. *There is no theoretical limit to the length of time that anything can remain in a state of non-dynamic, or potential, energy.*

However, if the clockmaker lets go of the pendulum, it will start to move, gradually getting faster and faster until it reaches the bottom of its swing. At this point it will be moving at its fastest. It will have maximum dynamic energy, and no potential energy left. All the potential energy will have been changed into dynamic energy. This point of no potential and maximum dynamic energy only lasts for an instant, exactly at the centre of the pendulum's swing. Then the pendulum will begin to slow down again as it climbs towards the top of its swing on the opposite side. When it reaches that point, it will stop again, for an instant, as it reverses direction prior to the return swing. It is at that stopping point that the pendulum's energy is once more all potential and no longer dynamic. Remember this instance of instantaneous stillness because we will return to it in a later chapter; it has great spiritual significance.

The swings continue ad infinitum, with the total energy of the pendulum changing from all potential at each end of the swing to all dynamic at the centre of the swing. In a perfect system with no friction and no air resistance, the pendulum would never stop swinging, and the energy interchange between potential and dynamic would always balance.

Now please consider the state of affairs which would exist if the clockmaker decided to stop the pendulum exactly at the end of a swing, at the instant when it is stationary between the up-swing and the next down-swing. If you had gone out of the room before the clockmaker first let go of the pendulum, before the very first swing, and you now returned, it would be quite impossible for you to tell whether the pendulum had ever swung at all. (Assume that the clock has no hands for this argument, so you cannot tell clock-motion by looking at the clock's hand-movement.) If you had come into the room while the pendulum was swinging, you would have been able to say with certainty that, at some time in the past, such and such an action had taken place, that is the clockmaker had started the pendulum swinging. But with no movement now taking place, and no apparent difference between the present state and the previous state, there would be no way of telling whether any action has taken place in your absence.

This scenario demonstrates that memory is part of the *dynamic* state of existence, and that a potential state does not necessarily contain any memories at all. Memory is dependent on time passing and *having been seen* to have passed. Memory has no meaning without time, and time has no meaning without memory. The two are totally dependent on each other. These statements are important when we look at what is 'happening' in the gaps in the Lattice.

Let's recapitulate at this point:

- All life is energy and all energy is life.
- Energy can be either active (dynamic), or waiting to act (potential).
- Absence of energy means absence of 'being', that is total non-existence.
- Memory is a function of time and does not exist where there is no activity (dynamic energy).

Each of these statements is important when it comes to understanding how the Lattice functions and therefore how life functions too.

The major point to note about the pendulum's moment of rest at the end of each swing is that all its future movement comes out of the potential energy contained in that resting state — that state of inactivity when the system is effectively at zero. If the pendulum were to be held at its mid-point and then released, nothing would happen because, having no potential energy to turn into dynamic energy, it would not move. Thus, not only does activity come out of non-activity, but the activity will only occur if the non-activity contains potential.

The remaining important characteristic of energy that should be noted carefully is that it cannot be lost or destroyed: energy can only be changed. It can be changed from dynamic to potential and vice versa. And it can be changed from one dynamic form to another dynamic form. From heat to light, to electricity, to the movement of water, to anything you can imagine, but it will always be the same total amount of energy. It can also be changed in form from animal to vegetable, to mineral, to thought, to emotion, to dream, and so forth. All these energy states are forms of life in its broadest sense, and they are all vibrations along the Lattice strings.

The final point to make in this important chapter is about Zero itself: it is that *all the potential of the universe is contained in the Lattice gaps*. This was said in another way at the beginning of the chapter where it was stated that Cosmos resides in the gaps of the Lattice. A statement such as this has far-reaching implications, which is why we are spending a lot of time making sure that all the descriptions about time, space and energy are fully understood.

In non-spiritual terms, the nothingness (Zero) between the Lattice strings is the source of all the dynamism from which we obtain Time, Space, and Life. In other words, the totality of the Universe comes out of this cosmic Zero. Because that Zero is itself timeless — being pure potential — it is impossible to imagine it in normal everyday terms. But one more simile may help to give some idea of what is contained within it.

Suppose that you are an intruder in a building which uses a modern burglar alarm system which senses movement. You managed to get in before the system was switched on and now, as long as you stay absolutely still and breathe very, very slowly, the alarm will not sense your presence. As far as the alarm is concerned, you are in a non-active state and therefore do not exist. It can only sense activity and therefore cannot sense you in your non-active state. But you yourself know that you do exist. Yours is a personal experience which cannot be communicated to anyone else without you becoming active in the process and thereby losing your Zero status. You are completely isolated from your surroundings as long as you stay in a non-active or Zero state. You can stay in this non-active state for as long as you like, knowing that you exist, even though the alarm is sure that nothing exists within its limited awareness. You are effectively in an eternal 'Now', just like the universe was before it exploded into the pattern with which we are familiar.

But as soon as you move, the alarm will sense movement and sound the alert. Its view of its restricted universe is that a miracle of spontaneous creation has just taken place. Nothing has suddenly become something. Where did this intruder come from? There was definitely nothing there; but now, all of a sudden, there is something there! The alarm does not understand what is meant by potential or non-active existence because it is only programmed to recognise activity. Non-activity is the same as nothingness. As far as it is concerned, there is only one state of life or existence: 'thereness'. 'Not-there' things do not exist in its 'understanding' of the universe; they cannot be recognised or even imagined. They can only be unacknowledged. *Similarly, the human mind can only comprehend existence related to a state in time.* It cannot understand or directly relate to a state of non-time or non-space. It sees all existence in terms of 'was, is, and will be' in a universe of 'here or there'; which is why we must try to understand about the timeless and spaceless Zero by simile.

Human beings have a great advantage over alarms and pendulums because we are connected to the 'Zeroness' of

Cosmos via an elusive substance (or non-substance) known as Spirit. We also have senses in addition to the five common time-space senses — sight, hearing, touch, taste and smell. Two of these extra senses are intuition and the underlying feeling of our connection with Cosmos. In modern society, these elusive senses are nearly always dormant because of the overwhelming number of signals we receive through the normal five. But they do still exist; and, hopefully by the end of this book, they will have woken again.

Once all the preliminaries concerning space, time, energy and Zero have been dealt with, we will be in a better position to look at the workings of our subtler energies and their interconnectedness with Spirit. And once we do that, we will also see how very closely linked together science and religion really are. The present mystique which seems to divide the followers of each from the other need no longer be a barrier.

Chapter 5

Moving the Energy About

We have come a long way in our understanding of the basic constituents of our universe, and this knowledge will be a great help in our journey. However, there are still a couple of things we need to look at. These are Time and Space. We've given a lot of attention to nothingness, non-time and non-space, so the natural conclusion is that we already understand about their opposites. Unfortunately, this is not necessarily true. Time and Space are two aspects of the universe about which we still know practically nothing. We know a great deal about the *effects* of time and space; but we know very, very little about the composition of these two phenomena themselves. Humankind has expended a great deal of energy over the centuries trying to understand them. Famous Greek philosophers such as Aristotle and Pythagoras spent much of their lives working out the laws of the structure of two dimensional space in their dissertations on geometry. (Geometry is Greek for the measurement of the earth.) Their ideas were expanded by mathematicians during the 19th and 20th centuries to cover topology —the mathematics of surfaces — and multi-dimensional space. But the composition of *space itself*, as opposed to its structure, remains largely unknown. Similarly, the Greeks devoted a lot of effort to discussions concerning the mechanics of time. Their ideas were also further expanded more recently following the publication of Einstein's Theory of Relativity, which gave us the term, 'space-time'.

Despite all these efforts by great thinkers, we still aren't sure if these basic constituents of the universe are continuous or occur in a series of jerks. This isn't really so surprising because time and space are such intrinsic components of our universe that we cannot consider either of them objectively, any more than a fish can really see or understand what water is. We cannot stand back and look at either time or space from the outside. All physical measurements have to include the observer and are therefore subjective. Imagine an inhabitant trying to describe a house purely from observations within one room.

According to the Theory of Relativity, neither space nor time may be considered in isolation; they must always be considered as one entity, space-time. From a physical point of view it is easy to see that there is a lot of truth in this hypothesis, and we do not need to be mathematicians or atomic physicists to understand the implications. Although relativity, particularly space-time, is usually considered to be something that only applies to space travel and atomic physics, it is something with which we are all concerned in our daily lives. Common sense and a little imagination will easily demonstrate that space and time are always interdependent.

Consider, for instance, a typical town, with typical roads, traffic and shops. Now imagine a typical car travelling along one of these roads, passing other cars, stopping at the traffic lights, etc. The cars which our chosen car passes in its journey in their turn pass other cars and other shops; the traffic lights at which our car has to stop also control the motion of other cars; the shops outside which our car may have stopped are also stopping places for other vehicles. So all the components of traffic and their positions in space are changing second by second: many cars are using the same points in space (for example, waiting at the traffic lights), one after the other.

Now imagine what the situation would be like if time ceased to exist. Everything would be at the instant, Now, and Now would also be Then, and Then would also be To Come. So our car would be passing *all* other cars at the same instant, 'Now'; and it would also be passing the traffic lights, stopping at shops and being parked in the garage all at this same instant 'Now'. No future or past occur in this scenario. All — everything and everywhere — occurs in 'Now' time. Thus the cars, traffic lights, shops, roads, garages, and everything else would all have to be squashed into the same point in space — the point where our car is. In a 'Now only' world, the whole town would be compressed into this single point in space. And the interconnecting roads to other towns would be at that same point in space also. The roads connected to other towns would rush to that single point, as would the outlying towns, cities, countries, oceans and, in fact, the whole world ! And this contraction of the world on one point would not stop there because the moon, sun, planets and stars would also come rushing headlong into it until, eventually, the whole universe would have contracted to a single point.

So, if time were to stop, it would automatically bring about the instantaneous contraction of space to a single point. *If there were no such quantity as time, there could not be any such quantity as space.* Time and space are co-dependent; neither can exist without the other. This is an important point. It is saying the same thing as one of the conclusions of Einstein's Theory of Relativity; but we have arrived there by a more mundane route.

To continue, if the cessation of time automatically brings about the contraction of space into a dimensionless state, then the reverse might also be true: *the commencement of time might automatically cause the expansion of space from a single point into the universe.* This would be the Big Bang beloved of modern scientists and discussed briefly in chapter 2. As the two are so tightly knit together, it is impossible to say whether time caused space to exist or space brought time into being. The reality is that they are actually two aspects of the same phenomenon, and neither 'exists' outside the mind of man. (More about this later.)

Going back to our earlier discussion about potentialism

(stillness) and dynamism (activity), we can now see that the compound term time-space is another term for movement. In order for something to move, both time and space must be involved. And, looked at from another point of view, if something is in time-space, it must be moving. As all life is in time-space, then all life must be moving. This is easy to see in the case of plants and animals, but is less obvious when looking at mountains and rocks. However, when these apparently static life forms are examined more closely, they can be seen to shimmer. The universe shimmers all the time. (Those people who take LSD or other psychedelic drugs can confirm this. In fact one of the definitions of psychedelic is 'dazzling in form'). Dr Fritjof Capra in his book, *The Tao of Physics*, describes his experience of seeing the 'rhythmic pulses' of energy coming down into matter. He explains that he saw the atoms of the elements and his body participating in this cosmic dance of energy. I have also observed this cosmic dance of energy during a state of heightened awareness on a country walk. The shimmering indicates life within the object. If the shimmering were to stop, it would mean that the object had moved outside time-space and would vanish. The shimmering would stop only because the energies of the Lattice had stopped, and nothing can exist in the Lattice strings except by virtue of its energy patterns.

The Lattice is truly infinite in that it is the structure into which space and time are placed. While scientists and astronomers argue about whether the universe has a boundary or not, the Lattice has no boundaries and continues to non-exist outside any material form we can possibly imagine. Inside the boundary of the universe most of the energy movements along the Lattice strings are experienced as real, or dynamic, happenings. Outside the boundary, (which is a physical one set by the limiting speed of light), there may be all sorts of alternative life-forms which are not controlled by the laws of physics with which we are familiar.

The basic idea of some sort of substance as a support for

the universe is not new. Both esoteric and scientific writings, particularly in the 19th century, discussed it. Blavatsky's *Web of the Universe* has already been mentioned. We have also mentioned the aether. This concept of aether fell into disrepute after an experiment conducted by Michelson and Morley in 1887 which was designed to demonstrate its existence or non-existence. The two scientists supposed that there must be an 'aether wind' created by the movement of the world through space, and they proposed to prove its existence by measuring the difference in the speed of light when a light beam was projected forwards and backwards as the world revolved on its axis around the sun. (The forward and backward speeds were expected to be different because of the Doppler effect). The result of their experiment was a complete surprise because they measured no difference at all. Although it did not conclusively disprove the existence of the aether, it led to the formulation of the Theory of Relativity. After this was published, the idea of an aether fell into disuse.

Similarly, in the case of the Lattice, no wind is created by objects moving through it because nothing *does* actually move through it: *all movements are vibrations within the Lattice itself*. The Lattice always remains stationary, and all motion we observe is actually movement of the patterns formed by the Lattice crossovers. All objects are fixed arrangements of these crossovers: when we think we see objects moving, what we are actually seeing are the crossover patterns moving as the energy waves move from one set of strings to the next.

This important principle of cosmic energy was explained in chapter 3, and illustrated by figures 1 and 2. What was not fully explained at that time is that there are many different types of vibration; some produce physical phenomena such as matter; some produce emotional phenomena such as anger or love; some produce mental phenomena such as ideas; and so forth. These different effects are caused by different types of the basic energy wave. A certain amount of interaction can occur between the differing energies, so that emotional waves can give rise to physical effects and vice versa. Note that emotional waves cannot directly cause physical patterning, but they cause sympathetic resonance of physical energy waves, and these can then create the physical effects.

In some cases, the energy patterns continue to exist for a long time and produce long-term effects such as planets and stars. Sometimes the patterns only exist relatively briefly, producing animal or vegetable matter. And sometimes they are very brief indeed, resulting in the momentary production of sub-atomic particles.

If we digress into the realm of conventional physics for a moment, this simplified picture makes it easier to understand the statement made in the Theory of Relativity: that is, that energy and matter are interchangeable, or are the same part of nature in different guises. The vibrational patterns of the Lattice, including its rate of vibration and the number of strings being vibrated, determine the size of the nodal lumps which physicists call mass. Thus the greater the amount of cosmic energy concentrated in one particular nodal area, the more we see the effect as an increase in the amount of matter at that point. Dependent on the manner in which the matter is being moved, it can be observed either as a simple movement of physical mass from one point in space to another, or as a change of mass back into energy.

Thus, the movement of matter from one point in space to another, (such as a car moving along a road), is actually the movement of the pattern of nodal points in the Lattice from one part of the Lattice to another. This seems to be a very complicated business and one might wonder why the parts of one car don't interchange with the parts of another car when they pass close by each other. But the system is very similar to many with which we are already familiar, such as the fact that two patterns of concentric circles of ripples in a pond will happily pass through each other and yet remain distinct. Similarly, two beams of different coloured light can pass through each other without becoming intermingled. This ability to remain separate and distinct in the presence of other similar systems of energy disturbances is possible because each system is generated as a *pattern*, not simply as a sequence of individual points. The Lattice registers the energy movements as distinct patterns and transmits those patterns faithfully. Thus, a car moving along a road is actually the movement of a complex pattern of energy nodes through the Lattice, each node being linked to the next by an invisible bonding pattern. The nodal patterns move, but the Lattice does not.

It is also important to realise that the energy wave which is forming a part of the pattern of a car at one instant may also be forming a part of the stalk of a leaf the next instant. Energy does not belong to any particular life pattern; it simply helps to form the patterns. This is similar to the fact that a beam of light does not belong to the thing it is reflected from; it simply interacts with that thing during the period of reflection. Then it moves on to illuminate something else. Once this characteristic of life patterns and Lattice energy is properly understood, some of the phenomena of magic and miracles become easier to comprehend. (See chapter 13).

Looking at scientific comparisons for a moment, the phenomenon of physical mass has a maximum rate of vibration along the Lattice of 300,000 kilometres per second, conventionally known as the speed of light. So when a mass tries to move through the Lattice at rates approaching this speed, the physical effect appears to be a growing mass. Meanwhile, the previous Lattice vibrations do not have time to move out of the way before new ones are being excited. So the vibrating nodes seem to bunch up and form a traffic jam. At the speed of light itself, the traffic jam becomes solid so that the energy required to move the mass becomes infinite. This agrees with the Theory of Relativity. In actual fact,

this infinite energy requirement is not true because resonances occur, just as they do for planes exceeding the speed
of sound. The possibility of moving faster than the speed of
light has not been acknowledged yet because conventional
thinking about light is contemporaneous with the thoughts
concerning aeroplanes before their travel exceeded the
speed of sound, that is, that infinite energy would be
required to cross the barrier. In fact, similar phenomena
occur at the speed of light and a 'luminant boom' would be
produced. This is futuristically portrayed in the *StarTrek* —
The Next Generation television series where, in the opening
sequences, the starship *Enterprise* gives off a luminant boom
as it accelerates beyond warp 1 (which is the speed of light
as far as that series is concerned).

The resonant energy requirement at the speed of light
does not apply to light itself because light is the basic
cosmo-physical vibration of the Lattice strings and does not
cause physical movement of the nodal-mass points. This is
where conflict occurs between the two schools of conventional thought regarding the composition of light. One
school says that light is a wave motion, while the other says
that light travels as bundles of photons. Both schools can
produce experimental evidence to back-up their theories. In
actual fact, the vibrations of the Lattice are wave-like in
nature; but they excite the crossover points of the Lattice as
they vibrate, thereby giving the appearance of moving bundles of energy. Thus, dependent upon how the physical
effects of the Lattice vibrations are observed and measured,
they are seen either as wave motions or photon-bundles.
These latter points are the bases of the Quantum Theory.
Other physical effects, such as laser light, can also be easily
explained using the model of the Lattice, but what has been
said is probably enough to show that such a model stands
up well to the tests of common sense and compatibility with
established physics.

It is important to understand that the Lattice exists continuously throughout the universe. There are neither breaks nor variation in structure. At all points and in all directions, it is basically identical. The variations which we see in space, such as planets, animals, mountains, seas, cheese-burgers, tennis racquets, etc., are the vibrational patterns of cosmo-physical energy waves moving through the Lattice. They exist in what we call the physical world and are normally subject to the limitation of the speed of light because that is the standard vibrational speed along the Lattice strings. The astonishing variety of physical forms possible from the interplay of these vibrations at different nodes is exactly the same as the infinite variety of sounds possible from the combined instruments of an orchestra: all the sounds are produced by simple vibrations of air, but the combined effects are for ever changing.

As already mentioned, vibrational patterns other than the physical ones are possible from other forms of the basic vibrational energy. Cosmo-physical vibrations produce physical manifestations. Cosmo-emotional vibrations produce emotional manifestations, which may be sensed as the 'emotional charge' emanating from an incensed crowd, or as the brooding air of desolation which hangs over areas where large-scale tragedies have occurred, for example the Glen Coe scene of a great massacre of the Scottish clans in the 18th century. Cosmo-astral vibrations can produce so-called psychic manifestations such as ghosts, poltergeists, and so on. And cosmo-mental vibrations can produce thoughts, telepathy, psycho-kinesis, etc.

Vibrational patterns such as telepathy, ghosts and psycho-kinesis are conventionally grouped under the banner of supernatural or paranormal. Until recently, they have been generally disregarded by the more intellectual members of humanity because they have been difficult to explain in everyday physical terms. For want of an easy life, we usually concentrate on those things with which we feel comfortable: the paranormal can be an uncomfortable part of our cosmic manifestations, especially for those among us who like to explain everything in physical or scientific terms.

The main reason for this inability to find satisfactory scientific explanations for a large number of events going on around us all the time is that today's humanity is pre-eminently concerned with just one small aspect of cosmic energy — electromagnetism. This energy has become the only thing that matters, with atomic forces and gravitational effects getting the odd look-in from the sidelines. These three form the bulk of cosmo-physical vibrational energy phenomena. They can be measured with intricate and highly accurate scientific apparatus and, being — to a large extent — predictable, are not threatening to the world at large.

Because modern science expects all measurements to be made by accepted means, the subtler energies of the Lattice, such as those used by dowsers and psychic healers, are said by conventional scientists and thinkers to be figments of the imagination. This is about as sensible as saying that electricity did not exist in the 15th century because the galvanometer had not been invented at that time and therefore it could not be measured. In fact, most of these subtler and so-called paranormal energies require a human interface in order to record them. For example, the divining rod requires a human operator to cause it to twist, and a dowsing pendulum requires a human operator to enable it to swing. And as these human operators are more prone to external changes than voltameters or weighing machines, the measurements made are liable to fluctuate. Thus, the experiments conducted around these homo-cosmic measuring devices tend to vary quite erratically, making it difficult to extract precise results or even say with any degree of certainty that today's positive results will still be positive when re-measured tomorrow. However, until we can find some substitute for the human constituent of these measuring systems, we will have to continue to work as best we can, accepting that these devices indicate the subtler vibrations of the Lattice. In a later chapter, we will show why it is necessary for human energy to be part of the paranormal measuring mechanism.

Having read this far, it will come as no surprise to learn that the many and varied vibrations within the Lattice move at different rates and have different limiting speeds. The cosmo-physical vibrations can move at up to the speed of light; the cosmo-emotional, astral and mental vibrations can move much faster. The cosmo-spiritual vibrations, (which is a blanket term for several higher-order vibrations), can move, for all intents and purposes, instantaneously throughout the universe. Thus, telepathic communication is much faster than electromagnetic radiation, and feelings of universal love, (which is a spiritual vibration), can flow from one side of the universe to the other in less than the blink of an eye.

Furthermore, any string of the Lattice can vibrate with a combination of several energy types at the same time. The various vibrations co-exist in each Lattice string just as happily as the sound vibrations of an oboe and a violin co-exist in the groove of a gramophone record without interfering with each other.

In fact, these relational effects are always taking place, although generally at a level which is too subtle for us to observe easily. For instance, it is often acknowledged that if you wish for something hard enough it will happen. And, surprisingly enough, it often does. This is an example of thought affecting matter. The mechanism of the transfer between the mental and physical planes is not understood by most ordinary people, but advanced beings such as Sai Baba have demonstrated countless times their ability to conjure matter out of thin air. (See chapter 13.)

This is the mechanism of miracles and it is accessible to all humankind. Like all good things, it has to be worked at and understood. And like all advanced techniques, (from driving a car to producing a perfect omelette), if the basic rule and proper procedures are not followed, a catastrophe can result and endanger the perpetrator. Spiritual energy is very powerful, and needs to be carefully controlled if it is to produce the desired result. A simple example is the use of healing energy by holistic practitioners who engage in 'hands-on' techniques such as reflexology or acupressure. They re-channel the body's higher life energies by touch and, in the process, can mix some of their own energies with those of the patient. If they do not prepare their minds and emotions carefully beforehand, and clean their energies properly afterwards, some of the transferred energy may 'stick', and then they themselves may become unwell.

At a more general level, the fact that interactions are not only possible but are the norm between the various planes of manifestation can give us a clearer picture of the way the universe works. The power of prayer is another good example — many people concentrating on a selfless action such as the curing of a child can make the healing happen. The pure thoughts of the people praying cause strong ripples in the mental plane, which generate corresponding ripples in the physical plane and thereby trigger the healing process.

People with 'green fingers' is another example of thoughts affecting physical things. Certain people are able to coax sick plants back to health and promote better growth from healthy plants. These people are said to be able to 'communicate' with the plants. They generally say that they 'talk' to the plants, which is another way of saying that they concentrate their thoughts and love towards the results they envision for the plants.

For the most part, natural healers, natural gardeners, and natural all-sorts-of-people do not really know how they achieve their minor miracles; they only know that they seem able to communicate their love and compassion to the object of their attention which is sick or feeble. Being aware of the mechanism of energy interchanges taking place between the Lattice strings does not help — any more than knowing the details of an internal combustion engine helps the average car driver. The point in briefly describing the mechanism here is so that you will become more aware that desires, thoughts, and feelings do not occur in isolation from what goes on physically in the world around you. Although the interchanges are generally small, in some cases they can cause very large and unexpected side effects; which may help answer the eternal cry, 'Why does it have to happen to me!'

To recapitulate: there is a Lattice-like structure throughout the universe and beyond, along the strands of which all the different energies of the universe pass as waves. At the crossover points of the Lattice, energy build-ups, called nodes, occur. We sense these nodes as mass, or electromagnetic force, or gravitons, or thoughts, or emotions, etc. These nodes form patterns which we recognise as physical, emotional, mental, paranormal or spiritual phenomena. The different energy waves travel along the Lattice at different speeds, and several can travel along the same strand at the same time without interfering with each other. The strands are so close together that even the most sophisticated measuring apparatus yet devised cannot accurately determine their spacing. By using the 'jiffy' as a yardstick, it is possible to estimate that there are probably 100 billion billion billion billion strands to the metre, where one billion equals one million times one million.

The full interplay between cosmic energies in the Lattice and humanity will be discussed later. At this point in our story, the most important aspect of the system to understand is that the energies of the Lattice represent life itself, in all its different guises. They all occur and exist simultaneously and we humans have the necessary sensitivity to perceive them all. However, because in modern life we tend to concentrate on the physical aspects of life energy, we often fail to sense these other vibrations passing along the Lattice, except as vaguely disturbing sensations. But these other cosmic vibrations are all there to help us on our path back to the Source.

Remember that this is the reason for this chapter and for this book. These descriptions of the Lattice and of time and space are here to help us understand what is *actually* happening around us. By now we should have a clear picture of all life linked together, from distant stars to flowers, from peoples all over the world to the animals they love or kill, from elegant penthouses in California to piles of stinking refuse in the back streets of Sao Paolo. Although it would be unrealistic to expect everyone to take responsibility for all that happens in the universe, it is necessary for us to realise that we have the capacity to rise to this level; that is to become aware of and accept our godliness.

In the succeeding chapters, we will continue to follow this theme by examining different types of Lattice energies in more detail, and seeing how their interactions create all the aspects of life with which we are familiar and a few which may be new to us.

Chapter 6

The Source Energy

Having discussed the meaning of non-existence, non-time, non-space, energy, time-space and spirituality, we can now look at how life emerged from the Zero state within the Lattice gaps and became manifest in humanity. This is another essential step on our path to understanding about ourselves and the purpose of our journey back to Cosmos.

Everything that ever was, or is, or ever will be has come out of the potential of the cosmic Zero. It is the fundamental state of Reality. It can be called God, Tau, The Way, Absolute Truth, or whatever else you like. In the simplest possible terms, and to remove any religious connotations which may cloud our judgments and interpretations of what is to follow, we decided in chapter 1 to call this source energy Cosmos. Cosmos is the originating source of every type of god you can think of and every type of god that there has ever been in the universe.

The previous chapters have already shown that Cosmos is beyond the understanding of our everyday existence because it is on the other side of Zero, the energy divide, in the basic non-time, non-space world of potential. (Remember that just like the burglar alarm in chapter 4, we are only programmed to understand active things, that is, things associated with time; and the energy of Zero is timeless.) The interesting facet of the concept of Cosmos-in-the-Lattice-gaps is that the energy of this Source is omnipresent in our dynamic universe. Nothing can get away from it because everything that exists must be part of the Lattice, and Cosmos is in all the gaps between the Lattice strings. Therefore this Source energy, this energy of creation, is an integral part of each one of us whether we be saint or sinner, president or peasant. We exist as Lattice energy patterns, as does the rest of creation, and we play out our lives against the background of the eternal Source filling the Lattice gaps which permeate us. So it can truly be said that Cosmos is an integral part of all things, including ourselves.

Whether we live or die, do good or evil, are happy or miserable, believe in a supreme being or are committed atheists, Cosmos will always be a part of each one of us; it always had been and always will be. There is no getting away from it. Wherever we go and whatever we do, to exist at a physical level we have to be in space and time. Thus we are full of Lattice gaps; and thus we are full of Cosmos! This is not a question of religious faith; it is a logical conclusion drawn from our previous discussion.

The god of the gaps is not the Jewish God, or the Christian God, or the Moslem God, or any other particular and exclusive God, *but the principle behind all ideas of personalised Gods*. The god in the Lattice gaps is beyond personalisation. It cannot be given any personality. It cannot be made a 'he' or a 'she', or be given human attributes such as jealousy, wrath, or even forgiveness because these are all personality traits and therefore involve 'beingness'. It cannot really even be referred to as 'it' because this word denotes objectivity; but as we have no other term to use, it will have to do. If we restrict our discussion to words which truly fit the Cosmic energy, nothing can be said at all because all words are limiting. This is why some Masters demonstrate the truth about the universe by silent communication. It is the only sure way to approach these ultimate mysteries. Cosmos is the Source from which all the energy in the universe comes. This is the place, or rather 'non-place', to which we are trying to return.

Contemplation of this ultimate energy takes us beyond the limitations of any religion or dogma into the realms of pure spirituality. All religions are to a greater or lesser extent limiting because they require some form of belief and demand some form of discipline. Cosmos demands nothing — it cannot by its very nature do so without becoming active and therefore dynamic. It is pure Source energy, so it cannot be held 'responsible' for anything. We cannot ask Cosmos to 'be on our side' as we fight our wars, or to 'punish the wrongdoer' when we ourselves have produced the laws which define what is right and wrong. Cosmos cannot be the partisan God of the Old Testament, or the exclusive God of dogmatic sects. The energy of Cosmos is absolutely pure and impartial. Being the potential from which all things come, it cannot be anything but totally unbiased. The human characteristics imposed upon the gods of all religions are man-made and form no part of the originating source.

This is the fundamental essence of spirituality as opposed to the man-made principles governing all religions. Pure spirituality is all-inclusive and beyond bias, whereas religions are by their very nature exclusive and discriminatory because they demand a belief in something or other. The only requisite of spirituality is a belief in one's own godliness — a belief in the ability of the soul to return to the Source. And this preferred requirement is not mandatory. All life is part of spirit whether that life-force acknowledges the Source or not. To be connected to spirit is simply a part of life, and there is no threat of eternal damnation for those who do not feel able to accept this fact.

While remembering that Cosmos is the potential, which exists throughout our dynamic universe, we should also remember that it can be transformed into active energy whenever we want that little bit extra. It cannot be exclusive, or unavailable to 'non-believers', as it is the motivating energy of the universe from which all else comes. Anyone who understands the mechanism of the Lattice energy transformation process can have immediate access to this infinite source of support. The transformation process can be initiated by prayer, attunement, meditation, etc. There is no set formula for its acquisition; the only requirement is a belief that it will happen. This is no different from riding a bicycle: it is the confidence that the bicycle will remain upright which enables the rider to maintain balance. Similarly, the confidence that spirit is there for the asking enables the correct links to be initiated and the spiritual energy to flow.

As the Lattice gaps are necessarily present and inter-connected throughout the universe and beyond, this means that Cosmos is literally omnipresent, existing in all places and in all things. It also means that Cosmos 'exists' outside the universe, because the Lattice continues past the boundaries of our universe. There is nothing miraculous or reverential in this concept: it is a simple logical conclusion inherent in the very concept of the Lattice. The energy patterns which form the universe stop at the boundaries of the universe because this is where time ceases to exist. But the Lattice goes on for ever and includes its gaps. Cosmos is in all the gaps; therefore Cosmos is present outside the universe.

The major obstacle in our journey back to the Source appears to be that we are dynamic, (because we are alive), whereas the Source is potential. Thus, there is an apparent energy barrier between us and the Source. Cosmos can transfer energy from itself into the dynamic universe, but the reverse process is not as easy. It is easy to get water to flow out of a pipe but much more difficult to direct water back into it. However, remember the pendulum: at the end of each swing, all the dynamic energy has become potential, just for an instant. This state of affairs occurs at the end of every swing. All human beings regularly pass through these 'instantaneous potential' points. But we do not notice them because we are unaware: we are asleep. One of the main purposes of Masters is to help us raise our awareness until we recognise these special times. (Then they carry us to the pool in the hope that we will recognise the reflected tiger.)

Most of us have some recognition of these points in our lives: those times when we instantaneously realise that everything makes sense. But they are so transitory that they have disappeared before we can hang on to them. 'Just for an instant everything was clear,' we say. 'If only I could remember, because just at that moment I knew what life was all about.' The reason why we don't remember these occasions, or the secret of life that was displayed for the instant, is because they are outside time. This has to be so because time is part of the dynamic universe, while the moments of 'instant potential' are necessarily part of non-time. Non-time has no memory. Therefore, the type of awareness we are seeking cannot be remembered; it can only be felt and lived.

A few paragraphs back, we talked about the soul, so now is a good time to look at the human make-up and see how the soul is associated with spirit. 'Soul' is a much misunderstood word — much as the word God is — because it is usually associated with religious experiences. But religion is not a necessary part of spirituality while the soul is a part of our spiritual being. Belief in Cosmos, spirit, or the soul, is not an essential requirement for reading this book. It is not designed to turn people into mystics and insist on a particular course of religious action. The following description of the soul and its place in the scheme of life is included in order to make the Lattice easier to understand.

In essence, the human soul is that part of each human being which is directly linked with spirit. It has no religious connotations; it is a purely spiritual device. Because it 'contains' spirit, (which is non-time and non-space), it cannot be exactly defined. So far as our journey is concerned, the soul can be considered to be the part of each of us which absorbs the essence of our experiences and feeds back an increasing awareness of reality. It is each person's individual and basic life-energy pattern in the Lattice. Other energies move through it and modify bits of it for a time, but there is a basic pattern which is unique to each soul — a sort of cosmic fingerprint.

Each human being has a unique and separate soul, and

this part of our being remains intact from life to life. (See the next chapter on reincarnation). In Eastern philosophies, the soul consists of three main parts — the Atma, or spiritual will; the Buddhi, or intuition; and the Higher Manas, or abstract mind. These three are also sometimes called the Ego, but this word is not synonymous with soul. Ego has a bias towards the second and third parts of the soul, while the soul itself is composed more of the first two. The rest of the human being is composed of the Lower Manas, or mentality; the Astral Being, or emotions; and the Etheric plus physical body. Above these six components of a human being is the Monad, or pure spirit. This is the aspect of us which connects directly with Cosmos and of which the greater part of humanity is unaware in its daily existence. The primary purpose of our journey is to increase our awareness of the Monad, because it is this which is our final link with Cosmos, and therefore our only way back to the Source.

In our earthly existence, in which we each suppose that we are separate beings, the soul is equated with individuality. The lower consciousness, emotions, and physical body form the personality. These two groups — the lower and higher selves — when combined with the spiritual essence beyond the soul, form the complete human being. By being aware of the function of each part, we will gradually become more aware of the spiritual aspects and move closer to the Source. In the end, we realise that only the spiritual part is real; all the rest is illusion. More will be said about this, (as it is the core of the mystical journey), after we have looked at the workings of reincarnation and karma in the next two chapters.

Before we do that, and as the final part of this chapter, we will look at another facet of human existence known as the chakras. This is partly to show how theory of the Lattice agrees with both spiritual as well as scientific traditions, and partly to show how the chakras connect body and soul

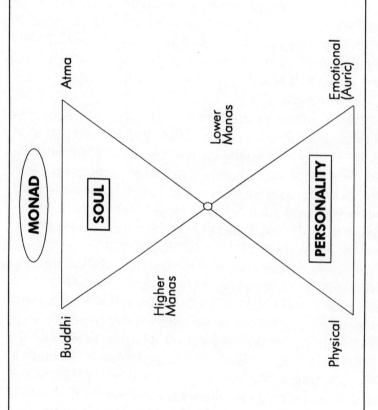

Figure 4. The Human Soul and Personality

together at a subtle level. Chakras are considered by occultists and many eastern religions to be the power centres of the human body. There are seven of them, situated at the base of the spine, at the reproductive organs, at the solar plexus, at the heart, at the throat, in the middle of the forehead just above the eyeline, and at the crown of the head. Sometimes they are referred to by number: counting the base chakra as the first chakra, the sixth chakra would the be the one at the forehead. Each chakra is responsible for particular functions of the human being, for example the solar plexus regulates the main bodily energy, while the chakra in the forehead is concerned with intuition, telepathy, and so forth.

These power points are not physically discernible because the energies they regulate are at a subtler level. They act through the ethereal body, which is a sort of invisible cloak worn by all humans and which contains the vital energies derived from the Lattice. This is the 'golden bowl' mentioned in the Bible, (Ecclesiastes 12:6). When it is 'broken at the fountain', it means that the physical body is dead and the ethereal energies are dispersing.

Some clairvoyants can see the ethereal body and there are descriptions of it in the works of people such as C W Leadbeater and Geoffrey Hodson. (Ref: the Theosophical Publishing House). As far as the Lattice is concerned, this is the main highway for the life forces in a human being, and the chakras are places where those energies are concentrated. The patterning of the human being is very concentrated at these points, with major interchanges between the various parts of the human make-up, such as the physical and emotional interchanges at the second and third chakras. Acupuncture meridians are the energy channels which take the diluted energy from the chakras, and the acupuncture points are where life streams cross at lower levels than those of the chakras. The whole system can be compared to a telephone system with the chakras corresponding to major exchanges.

When the chakras are perfectly balanced, life energy flows unimpeded through all seven, allowing all the different bodies which make up the human being to resonate in perfect accord with the originating Cosmic signals. This is the ambition of many mystics; but the path is fraught with danger because the energies become more powerful as they near mutual resonance. If the person is not absolutely ready at all levels, this force can shatter many of the Lattice patterns, resulting in madness, heart failure, cancer, or paralysis. A few impatient travellers try to take short cuts by practising dangerous exercises such as those based on 'raising Kundalini'. Kundalini is the eastern name for the quiescent energy located in the base chakra, and it should not be disturbed until the other two chakras below the heart are purified and balanced. Once this is achieved, Kundalini starts to rise of its own accord; but if it is forced, excessive energy can be taken from higher chakras and disaster is the usual result.

No practices of this sort are recommended in this book. Our watch-words are patience and awareness. Remember that a great deal of the purpose of this journey is to take delight in it — and always remember to smell the wayside roses !

Chapter 7

Reincarnation

The normal way for human beings to become life patterns in the Lattice is by being born. Before this process takes place, the substance of each human soul must already exist. It originally came into existence when the Cosmic source energy bridged the energy boundary and manifested itself at the spiritual level. Each soul has been a part of a human being many times before and contains the essence of the lessons of our previous lives. This is the principle of reincarnation. Nowadays more than half the population of the world believes in reincarnation in one way or another. It is simple, logical, and in accord with the principle that energy cannot be destroyed; it is also in no way incompatible with Christianity. Buddhists, Hindus, Jains and Sikhs all believe that more than one life is necessary in order to achieve their ideas of perfection and return to the Source. Buddhism alone accounts for about 25 per cent of the world population. As we shall see, the philosophy of multiple lives helps to explain such riddles as God's supposed callousness in allowing the apparently wasteful and unnecessary deaths of babies, and the starvation of millions during famines in Third World countries. Knowledge of the reincarnation mechanism does not reduce the grief of parents who lose a baby, but it should ease the loss and thereby lessen the long-term trauma of separation.

Once upon a time, the Christian church also accepted the idea of reincarnation; but this acceptance was rejected after a few hundred years. St Clement of Alexandria, St Gregory of Nyssa, St Jerome, and Origen all wrote positively about reincarnation between the 2nd and 4th centuries. Then, after the second council of Constantinople in 553, Christian belief in reincarnation was forbidden by order of Emperor Justinian.

This was a political move which had nothing to do with religious doctrines and was not approved by the Pope at the time. (It is believed that he was actually being held captive by Justinian, and was therefore unable to attend this important council meeting). Nevertheless, key figures in Christianity continued to accept reincarnation as a reasonable doctrine, including St Francis of Assisi (1182-1276) and the Franciscan cardinal, St Bonaventura (1221-1274). Even today, there is strong evidence that reincarnation is accepted by more people in Britain than those who accept traditional Christian teachings: 12 per cent as opposed to 10 per cent according to a 1955 study made by Geoffrey Gorer in *In Search of English Character*. Since then, the proportion has almost certainly increased further.

Stated simply, the theory of reincarnation says that each soul has to journey back to the Source via a series of physical lives. The actions performed in each life time are a help or hindrance to further progress, and the lessons learnt are assessed in the pauses between lives in order to determine what needs to be learnt next. Gradually, over a period of thousands of years and hundreds of lives, the soul becomes more aware of its Cosmic (godly) origin and thereby draws nearer to the Source, (which we know from previous chapters to be the potential energy from which all things come). It is not possible to cross the Zero barrier and return to the Source until all the energies that make up a human being have been balanced exactly and the action/reaction cycle of human life totally replaced by the pure potential of spirit. This balancing action is called the Law of Karma and is explained in the next chapter.

The above is a simplified explanation of reincarnation and different religions have introduced many variations on the basic theme. Some Hindus believe that retrogression is possible for people who commit evil acts and that they can revert to animal, or even plant, life. Buddhists do not believe in a soul but in the five Attributes which contain a person's cravings. These attributes, or Skandhas, continue after a person's death until he destroys them by losing the cravings. Thus they incorporate the basic energies from one life to the next in the same way as the soul. And there are many other variations, but they are all based on the understanding that each human needs more than one life in order to achieve perfection.

The process of incarnations started long before humanity existed, because souls originally evolved from a general cosmic 'soup' by gradually separating into individual nodal Lattice patterns through the mineral, vegetable and animal kingdoms. In the earlier stages of pre-human life, the soul energy was still in group form, as is still the case with most forms of life. Only human beings are totally individualised. The Cosmic energy feeding the 'soul core' of lower life structures produces communal patterns embracing large numbers of mountain, cabbage, or ant Lattice nodes. Even domestic animals receive their spiritual energy in group form, although they are almost completely separated from each other by this stage in the evolutionary process. (Note how shoals of fish and flocks of birds seem able to communicate with respect to actions such as the instantaneous change of travel direction by the whole group).

The change from higher-order animal to human life is the change from a group Lattice pattern to an individual soul pattern. This occurs when an individual within the group becomes sufficiently aware of its own identity to develop a personality and thereby trigger the separation mechanism. It is then seen in the energy patterns of the Lattice where the spiritual energy nodules leave the group field and take on a unique pattern peculiar to the newly evolved human being. Once this separation has happened, it cannot revert to group patterning and the individualised pattern remains unique to that soul throughout its incarnations.

It is therefore worth remembering that at some time in the distant past, we were each part of a herd of animals, and before that, a part of a forest, and before that, a part of a river or mountain. (Remember the comment in an earlier chapter that our constituent molecules were once part of distant stars). This should help us to feel more affinity with the other life forms of this planet, whether they be human, animal, vegetable or mineral, and to be more concerned with the proper nurturing of our environment and its resources. Even though we are now individualised, we are still strongly connected to our origins by the Lattice strings. The death of a salmon in the acidic waters of a Scandinavian lake actually causes a minute modification in our individual vibrational patterns. All these other forms of life are truly parts of our own family.

When the world we live in at the moment becomes full of incarnating souls, there will be plenty of other worlds for them to go to in this universe. Remember that the restrictions of the speed of light only apply to the physical realm and the physical vibrations of Lattice energy. Soul energy is massless and can easily move between solar systems almost instantaneously. But once incarnated on a particular planet, a soul is then bound to the environment of that planet until initial enlightenment* is reached; that is, it cannot incarnate on Alpha Centaurus and then move after a dozen lives to the planet Earth. This would create too much confusion in the inherent subconscious memory which we each take from life to life, and the sympathetic vibrations between the different energy levels of each soul do not allow it.

At first sight the laws of karma and reincarnation seem to

---

*Enlightenment is that evolutionary stage where the soul becomes fully aware of its godly origins, not just as theory, but as incontroversial fact. There are different levels of enlightenment, ranging from the guru with basic spiritual awareness up to the world teachers with total awareness of the true meaning of existence on the other side of the Potential barrier. To become enlightened does not mean that the 'journey' is finished! Rather, it is somewhat like moving from lower to upper school, with more advanced souls as prefects and then as university undergraduates.

be quite straightforward, but they are sometimes interpreted by sceptics and critics too literally. For instance, it is sometimes thought that if you harm a horse in this life, then in your next life you and the horse will change places so that the horse can hurt you. This is too facile. The law of reincarnation does not allow retrograde transmigration in this way. (Some teachings refute this, but interpretations differ and modern translations are increasingly in favour of non-regression. As has already been said, the theory of the Lattice does not support a return from individual to group patterning). Once the soul's energy has separated from the general group and been vibrated with a personalised human patterning, it will always re-incarnate as another human being, whatever the harm it has perpetrated on other life forms. It can never revert to a group format again, although excessive cruelty or other forms of negative energy will cause it to have a heavy karmic debt to discharge before it can move forward. Ultimately the soul comes to terms with the fact that it has been using energy in the wrong way and a natural progression towards perfection can start again.

The time during which the soul contemplates its progress or lack of it in a particular life is usually during the periods between each life: that is, the periods between incarnations. At each death of a human body, a particular part of the Cosmic field ceases to feed energy to the soul for a while. In biblical terms, the silver cord is loosed and the pitcher is broken at the fountain (Ecclesiastes 12:6): this is just a description of the way in which psychics see the stream of human life energy receding from the deceased, and the solar plexus chakra ceasing to resonate.) The soul energy still exists as a pattern in the Lattice, but the physical life energy vibrations are missing. During this non-life period, the patterns of the recently ended existence are studied and compared with the long-term soul energy required for karmic balance. According to the outcome of this assessment, a decision is made as to the best sort of life in the next human existence

— one in which to move closer towards perfection. The soul has a fairly free choice in this decision, so that it can opt for, say, three 'easy' lives, one after another. But this hedonistic policy will lead to such an imbalance in the general energy pattern eventually that the only course left would be to have a few really 'difficult' lives to compensate for those previous easy times. This explains why, for some people, nothing in life ever seems to go right, while others are born with the proverbial silver spoon in the mouth.

This process of life-death-analysis goes on for hundreds and hundreds of times. Sometimes the human life energy remains in one nodal pattern for 70 or 80 years; sometimes it remains for only a few minutes. But each time the life pattern is formed, for however long or short a time, further essential experiences of the cosmic energy patterns are absorbed by the soul. This explains why babies sometimes die at or before birth. These help to modify and improve that individual soul's overall cosmic energy balance. It is also worth mentioning at this point that incarnating souls are not necessarily always born for their own progress. Occasionally, a soul will act as a catalyst for another soul's advancement. In such a case, a baby may live for only a few minutes, not for its own karmic development but as a help to the mother's soul energy or someone closely related. Although the lessons and circumstances often appear hard when viewed in isolation, the broad view, when taken over a longer period of time, usually shows that spiritual progress has been made.

It is perhaps one of the hardest lessons for human beings to learn that spirit is not so concerned about any individual human life that it would want to preserve it above all else. Human beings, by virtue of their close affinity to the personality triangle, see death as a major catastrophe — and, for that particular personality, it is of course because it then ceases to exist. But, just like John Brown, the 'soul goes marching on'. The soul is the important part of the human being and it is where the energies concerning the lessons of life are stored.

The process of incarnating again and again can be compared in some ways to the buying and selling of cars. The soul uses human bodies as vehicles, much as people use their cars. During a lifetime, one person may change cars many times; just as throughout its total existence, a soul will use many bodies. Nor does it not become overly attached to a particular body any more than an average driver becomes overly attached to a particular car. Cars are for convenience; and so are bodies. When a car has served its purpose or becomes too decrepit, it is replaced; and the same goes for the human body. A little mourning for the demise of a favourite car or body is to be expected, but then it is time to arrange delivery of the replacement.

In considering the interaction of life forces, the Lattice can be envisaged as an enormous billiard table with no pockets; it is covered by millions of different coloured billiard balls. Each ball represents an energy pattern in the Lattice. Once in the past, all the balls were stationary, representing the universe before time began. Then, at the commencement of time, a ball was shot into the middle of the table and all the other balls started moving in different directions as they collided with one another. As there is no friction or air resistance to be considered in this theoretical model, there is nothing to stop the balls from moving continually about the table, colliding with each other and the cushions. The movements apparently can go on for ever, forming different patterns, with the balls taking energy from, and giving energy to, each other. Each energy interaction obeys the law of cause and effect, so that the overall energy on the table is always the same. Thus it can be said that each ball acts as a carrier for the original energy derived when the first ball was first shot onto the table. Theoretically, it is possible at some time in the future for a mirror set of movements to occur, with the original initiating ball leaving the table, thereby causing all the remaining balls to become stationary once more. Imagine that the Creation was recorded on video and that the tape is being replayed backwards. The injection of dynamic energy which was first given to the system by the active ball is now taken back by that same ball, and only potential energy remains.

This is what happens, on a smaller scale, in our incarnations. We each have a pattern of energies forming our lives, like the balls on a personal billiard table. Every now and then the initiating ball comes or goes from that table. During the rest periods, when time is 'standing still', we each examine the frozen pattern of the balls remaining and decide on the best place, direction and speed for the reintroduction of the initiating ball so as to obtain the required result during the next period of play. The conclusion reached then determines where, when, and with which parents we will be reborn in order to facilitate the right energy balance in the next life.

The movement of the balls on the table can obviously be very complex and the decision concerning the place of the initiating ball does not always bring about the desired result. Ultimately we will each position the balls on our table in the correct positions, bearing in mind that the more lives we have, the more experience we will gain in pattern recognition and prediction; however, it is quite natural that we feel that little progress is being made for quite long periods of time. Like playing the piano, practice makes perfect even though it can be hard work and quite boring at the start.

From the above analogy, we can be see that because the ball patterns are continuous from one life to another, it is possible for 'aware' people to recognise their patterns from one life to the next. Generally this degree of awareness is not necessary as it is the energy interchanges *during* that life which are important in forming the pattern for the next one. Past life energies are only relevant in that they helped form the starting pattern for that particular life. However, in special circumstances, a knowledge of some of the past energies can be helpful in determining the best arrangement of those energies with which to leave the table set for the next rest period. This is especially true for souls who are stuck in a particular pattern which is unhelpful in enabling them to learn the lessons they originally decided upon. Past life regression therapy or the help of a Master will show the pattern clearly so that the human can take appropriate action to overcome his or her handicap.

The actions and reactions of the various forms of cosmic energy obey the rule that the total energy of any system can only be transformed, but never increased or diminished. Thus it is possible to move energy from the physical to the mental plane and vice versa. Generally, the movement of energy from one plane to another, such as the physical to the mental, results in an apparent lessening of the amount of energy present. This is due to the energy transfer by sympathetic vibration, in the same way that the sounding of a C note on a piano will cause the other C strings to resonate, albeit at a lesser level, plus its harmonics such as the G note at the interval of one fifth above the sounded C.

When we eventually come to understand that these interchanges are going on all the time to everyone and everything, and that they are the basis of cosmic existence, we will then be in a position to use them consciously as a help to ourselves on our journey. Knowing that we are each composed of the basic energies of the four planes — physical, emotional, mental and spiritual — and that we can interchange these energies according to certain rules, we can then begin to regulate our lives whilst taking these new factors into account. We can start to become masters of our energies rather than letting them rule us. That, after all, is a reasonable aim in life. Even if we do not expect to govern our providence rather than having it govern us, at least it would be nice to treat it as an equal once in a while! This change-over from servant to friend is by no means instantaneous; theory and practice are, as usual, a long way apart. The process of change is similar to learning to drive a car: the theory may well be understood; but the reality of holding a steering wheel while changing gear, and simultaneously negotiating along the road without hitting kerbs, people, or other vehicles requires a great deal of practice.

How do we practice the business of becoming proficient at using the subtler energies of the Lattice? Our day-to-day lives are governed by the coarser energies that control normal physical, emotional and mental functions. These functions are available simply to keep the 'vehicle' going — to allow the body to operate efficiently. The subtler energies such as intuition and spiritual awareness are available to help us move closer to the boundary between dynamic and potential existence. In order to make good use of these energies, we need to bypass logic because logic keeps us time-bound. Thus we need to slow down our mental processes. For many hundreds of years, the traditional means of quietening the mind in India and many eastern countries involved the practice of various forms of yoga and meditation. The western body and mind are less able to adapt to either of these disciplines, and most westerners give up after just a short foray into the unfamiliar disciplines. Eastern minds are generally more open than western ones. Western minds tend to be more inquisitive and are always 'on the go'. This can make meditation difficult. However, western equivalents to meditation can be found in the form of prayer and attunement. These give the non-time energies such as intuition a chance to be heard.

The western approach to becoming proficient in the use of the Lattice energies often begins more with reading rather than discipleship. This is necessary to satisfy the inquisitiveness of the occidental mind. Eventually the reading is reinforced by practical action as the seeker goes to places which offer functional courses in spiritual disciplines — such as the 'New Age' communities springing up throughout the western world and Australasia. After a time, one set of answers is replaced by another; and, if the seeker is moving well along the path, the time will come when the futility of both questions and answers will be realised, and the western inquisitiveness will come to terms with eastern acceptance.

Hand in hand with the ability to accept a teaching without full knowledge of its likely effects goes the necessity to take risks. Once again, the eastern temperament is generally more attuned to taking risks, trusting to fate with regards to the correct outcome for the particular atman. This ability to accept stems mainly from an ingrained belief in the workings of karma and reincarnation. If cause and effect are always working and balancing one's life, how, asks the oriental mind, can any spiritual catastrophe occur? Short-term physical catastrophes may happen, and the physical body may perish in the process, but the soul must always benefit. This is not to say that human life is considered as totally unimportant by the eastern mind, however since each life is accepted as but one of many, the emphasis on staying alive at all costs is not so pronounced. What one does with one's life is more important than how long it will last. In other words, quality is more significant than quantity.

Another aspect of the theory of reincarnation is worth mentioning before we move on to consider karma: as we need to learn different sorts of lessons, it is necessary for us to live our series of lives as a whole variety of human beings. Thus, one is sometimes male and sometimes female; sometimes westerner and sometimes easterner. It is helpful to see the patterns of each life from different points of view, so it is often the case that a group of souls will keep together for a series of lives. The father and daughter in one life may become the niece and uncle in the next, and then a married couple in the one after that, and so forth. This grouping does not go on for ever; combinations change as lives go by, just like friends change within a lifetime. It helps to account for those strange meetings where a person says to someone they have just met, 'It's funny, but I feel I have known you for years. I feel so *comfortable* with you'. And then, at other times, a person meets someone against whom they feel instant antagonism. In this case, it is probably a soul who has chosen to act as a 'karmic hurdle' which needs to be overcome as part of a particular lesson.

Looked at from the scientific point of view, reincarnation is a natural extension of the precept that energy cannot just vanish, rather, it has to become another form of energy. And looked at from the spiritual point of view, reincarnation is the natural way for the soul to progress towards perfection. It is a pity that western religion 1,500 years ago got involved with politics and decreed that the idea of soul progression from life to life is untenable. The probable purpose of this denial was to introduce a scheme whereby the church of the time would have had more control over its congregation. The terrors of Hell are far more meaningful if there is only one life to be lived. And it is then a small step to suggest that those people who disobey the dictates of the Church will be damned for ever. Hence, the collection of monies for church funds and the blind obedience of parishioners to the bishop and his priests would be assured. These reasons for a denial of reincarnation no longer apply, but the tradition of a single life for all beings has become the norm of the western religious message.

Chapter 8

Karma

The word 'karma' is Sanskrit for 'works'. It is loosely translated as fate, which generally makes us think that the world
is against us; whereas karma does not involve any form of
judgment. The Law of Karma states that all karma, (our
works), is reaction to the situations we create ourselves. It is
an automatic process which cannot be side-stepped. 'As ye
sow, so shall ye reap.' This is not a statement that punishment is the lot of the wrongdoer and pleasure the reward of
the righteous; rather that all actions will eventually bring
upon the perpetrators equal and opposite reactions in accor-
dance with the basic balancing system of the universe. We
ourselves impose the 'good/bad' judgment on events: in
actuality all events are simply energy movements within the
Lattice. The whole universe is a perfectly balanced system
with a fixed amount of dynamic energy in it, so anything we
take must eventually be put back and anything we give will
eventually become ours again. We have no choice in the
matter except in the timing of the interchanges (just like the
billiard balls mentioned in the last chapter cannot decide not
to move when they are hit).

This rule of balance applies at every energy level. At the
physical level, Newton has formulated it as his third law of
motion:'for every action there is an equal and opposite reaction'. This simple law observes that is the reactive force of
the ground opposing the pushing action of your feet which
gives you the impetus to move forward as you walk along
the street. Thus, you can't walk on ice unless you increase
the reactive force by using studs in the soles of your boots.

At the emotional level, this opposing force can be seen as
a natural reaction to strong fear, which is the need to laugh.
Shakespeare was a past master at exploiting this human trait

and did so brilliantly in *Macbeth* for instance, where he introduces the comic relief of the drunken porter immediately after Duncan's brutal murder. Without some sort of safety valve for the reactive forces, the audience would become restive and lose concentration.

At the mental level, reactive forces can be seen as the need for total relaxation of the mind after periods of intense thought, such as Sherlock Holmes playing his violin between bouts of crime-solving. It is now well known by school teachers and university lecturers that short periods of intense teaching interspersed with relaxing breaks produce better memory retention by the students than longer teaching periods and longer breaks.

At the spiritual level, it is more difficult to see the simple pluses and minuses in the equation because we tend to confuse spirituality with religion, labelling some religious experiences as 'good' and others as 'bad' dependent on our upbringing and moral stance. In fact, a great part of religious dogma has more to do with emotions and social acceptability than with spirituality. The do's and don'ts of the average church were originally constructed to keep the community safe and healthy rather than to ensure the congregation's travel heavenward! This is because, until recently, the Church and the State were closely interwoven and it was a natural process for constitutional and canon law to overlap.

At its most basic level, the energy of spirituality remains constant and indivisible. Cosmos makes no qualitative judgments about it at all: judgments are only made at the human level and only human beings have a sense of good and bad. This is an important point as it puts into perspective many of our fears about 'doing right' and not 'doing wrong'. The actions which are approved of today may be against the law tomorrow, and vice versa. But, as far as Cosmos is concerned, nothing is ever approved or disapproved of. All that happens is that each time a part of the system is moved out of balance, it will naturally try to balance itself again. We may call the unbalance 'evil' and the rebalancing 'good', (or vice versa), but the reality is that we impose these moral judgments simply to ensure that we — as individuals and the community as a whole — appear to suffer as little as possible. Our judgments have no cosmic significance, and they cannot affect the karmic outcome.

The karmic process of returning-to-balance cannot be bypassed or cheated. It is absolutely fundamental to the cosmic scheme. There is no way that a bargain can be struck with the devil or a good fairy in order to change the final balance of fate. (People who try to use these methods usually lose out in the end anyway: for example, Dorian Gray and Faust). This is not to say that everything is preordained and that there is no such thing as free-will. The re-balancing process can be modified by our actions so as to take a longer or a shorter time, or to generate a more or a less intense experience. We can, metaphorically speaking, go from London to Birmingham via the M1 motorway or follow G K Chesterton's *Rolling English Drunkard* and take a route via Beachy Head. Whichever route we take, we will eventually end up in Birmingham. That is how the certainty of karma and our gift of free-will interact with each other. The choice of route is ours; the destination is preordained.

This karmic cycle of cause and effect cannot end until perfect balance has been re-established — which is the ultimate object of the exercise. Until that time, each action will *always* cause a reaction, and each reaction will always cause a further reaction, and so on. Often the reaction is not an obvious one, although it is always there. The cycle is equally true for both individuals and the universe; it started when time-space came into existence, and it can only be stopped when a perfect balance of timelessness is restored, that is when Creation returns to a state of pure potential. When things eventually return to this state, there will be absolutely no dynamism left: not a single grain of sand left on the seashore; not a single echo of a sound left in the wind. All types of manifestation involve dynamism, or life, and perfect balance requires only potential and no dynamism.

Luckily for us humans, we do not need to wait until doomsday in order to achieve individual perfection. That can be done by our arrangement of our personal action/reaction process so that it comes to its own point of balance. This might be an easy thing to say, but a very long and involved process to achieve finally. Thankfully, a knowledge of the workings of the Lattice and cosmic energy can help the process.

Since it is often difficult to catch the action/reaction process taking place, this can easily mislead us to believe that it doesn't always happen. Often the reaction has occurred in a different energy form from that of the originating action. A simple example of this in the physical plane is the conversion of chemical energy from a torch battery into electricity (in order to heat a torch-bulb filament) and then into light. The light illuminates objects which reflect the light back into the observer's eye, where it is re-converted into chemical energy in order to operate the nervous system feeding information to the brain. So a chemical-electrical-heat-light-chemical action/reaction chain has been triggered in this simple example. All energy action/reaction chains follow similar lines. Very seldom does a process remain within the same form of energy throughout its operation.

Similarly, action/reaction patterns occur between the physical, emotional and mental levels. A slap on the face, (physical), may cause anger, (emotional), which may cause ideas for revenge, (mental), which may cause retaliation, (emotional), in the form of a kick to the shins, (physical). Or the slap, (physical), may cause depression, (emotional or suppressed anger), which may cause a stomach upset, (physical).

These are fairly obvious examples; but often the reactions are very obscure and can only be seen to be associated with the originating actions many years later, if they are ever observed at all. This is especially true of suppressed emotional reactions which hide away in the subconscious and give a lot of interesting and lucrative work to psychoanalysts.

Often the reactions to a set of events may not occur until a later life. In fact, the whole point of reincarnation is to allow the unbalanced energies from one life to be sorted out in another. When I was quite young — about 11 years old — I came to the conclusion that, as energy cannot be destroyed, the unfinished energy patterns of one life have to be worked out by the soul returning to another body in a future life. It was not until I was 18 that I came across the theory of reincarnation. My private theory of energy balance was purely the result of looking at things from an engineering point of view. Thus, to my way of thinking, reincarnation and cosmic energy exchanges are complementary systems. Very seldom is it possible for a life style to be chosen by an incarnating soul which will satisfy all the karmic situations arising during that particular life. Frequently, the reactions to actions arising during a masculine life need to be experienced during a subsequent female life and vice versa. Likewise, experiences gained in situations of poverty may need to be reacted to in a lifestyle of abundance; a healthy body in one life may need to be followed by a sickly one, and so forth.

The cycles of cause and effect at all levels of manifestation originally start a special energy based on polarisation. Polarisation is the energy which initiates differences. Positive polarises with negative; high with low; in with out; etc. All energies can be split into opposites except for the originating spiritual energy since it is essentially sparked from the originating cosmic Source, which has no opposite. Without opposites, there can be no reaction to an action; no effect to a cause. Polarisation is the process by which the originating unity splits into a duality. It is the most important division of energy in the Lattice system because it is the start of all manifestation processes. It is the primary creative principle available to all life forms. Without this energy of polarisation, or difference, any creative process can only be the result of parthenogenesis, in the same way that Spirit is a division of Cosmos.

It is interesting to note that in many major religions, and in the ancient myths of Scandinavia and the Mediterranean, the first divine beings were supposed to have come into existence directly from an omnipotent source. Thus they came into being by parthenogenesis, rather than from a normal male/female or this/that type of relationship. This concept accords with the Lattice theory that all life originally came from Cosmos through the non-polarised energy of Spirit.

Consider a few examples of the parthenogenetic origins of the universe, as set down by ancient thinkers. The Olympian myths of ancient Greece say that Ge, the Earth Mother, gave virgin birth to the father of all the gods, Uranus. Ge herself simply emerged from Darkness. Uranus then fathered the Titans through a liaison with his own mother, Ge. (This incestuous relationship neatly side-steps the problem found in Genesis where Cain, as one of the three sons of the only other two people in existence at the time, (Adam and Eve), manages to go off to the east of Eden and marries a girl from Nod. How did she happen to be around if Eve was the only woman alive?).

Both the Homeric and Orphic myths from ancient Greece suggest that the Creation was the result of a union between Chaos and the wind, Boreas. These myths are interesting reading because they can be seen as early attempts to establish a comprehensive system for the origin of all things, before normal impregnation and birth processes existed. Scandinavian mythology acknowledges a supreme existence *before* Chaos. The giant of Chaos emerged from the pre-chaotic state and gave existence to the world, the heavens, and the gods from various parts of his corpse after he was slain by the three brothers, Spirit, Will, and Holiness. (This is very similar to the Egyptian story of the god Set). It is also interesting to note in passing that Spirit, Will, and Holiness are translations of the three aspects of the monad mentioned in chapter 6.

In early Hindu writings, Krishna is supposed to have come into existence by virgin birth, and the same process is repeated in Christianity for the birth of Christ.

In all these cases, the emergent god-like being was not the result of a normally polarised male/female unification process; thus, the general rules of karma do not apply, and it could be said, in Christian parlance, that the being was born 'without sin'. In more general terms, this rather puritanical phrase simply means that the being would have the capability to return to the non-existent state without having to go through the process of karma and the wheel of fate. As no polarising action was involved in the being's creation, no reaction would be required at the cessation. Thus, the being could be said to be already perfect or enlightened. (This is a difficult statement to accept when one looks at the skulduggery apparently perpetrated by the gods of old. However, we must remember that most of the stories contained in the myths have been considerably embellished so as to make them more interesting to the bloodthirsty listeners of those times. Only the essence of each myth can be taken to have any real meaning, and then it should still be compared with corresponding myths from other cultures for reliability).

Looked at logically, once the energy of polarisation emerged from Spirit and produced the very first reaction, all subsequent actions must then be reactions, since no further 'virgin' action would be possible. In other words, after the originating cause, everything which is not purely spiritual has to be an effect of that cause. This gives us a new way of looking at the eternal problem of sin and what we do about it. The accepted purpose of karma is to become sinless: to balance one's sins with good deeds and hence attain enlightenment. From the cosmic point of view, sin is just another way of saying that we can never act in an original manner, that we are only programmed to react. Sin is simple reaction. Our way out of this impasse is to become aware of the cosmic origins of all manifestation: we need to become aware of inherent Spirit.

The word 'sin' probably comes from the Latin 'sontis' or the German 'sünde', meaning 'guilty of having done something'. So, originally, a guilty person was someone who had 'done something' and was required to pay a fine. (The word 'guilt' comes from gylt or gold). Thus although a 'sinner' was someone who had transgressed and needed to balance his or her misdeeds with a payment to the community, sin as such was not considered a major evil. Later on however, Christian theology proclaimed that 'man was born in sin', and this degenerated further into the doctrine of 'original sin' and Adam and Eve's fall from grace in the Garden of Eden. What all this is really saying is that the devolution of actionless Spirit into reactive life-forms has introduced mankind to a continuous reaction process from which it is difficult to escape. All reactions produce further reactions, so the way forward is not by action but by becoming more aware.

It is our human judgments which say that such and such an action is 'good' while another action is 'bad', and these judgments vary according to the needs of society. Otherwise, why is it acceptable for a girl to marry at the age of 12 in some parts of the world, but not in others? Why do some cultures regard alcohol as an evil but accept drugs, while others reverse the taboos? There are thousands of similar examples. They show that human sin is a relative, and not an absolute, state. Even the Ten Commandments are subject to interpretation and depend upon circumstances. They were originally concocted with the well-being of the tribe in mind, because Moses was primarily a law-maker. (This is another example of Church and State as common authority). Thus, sin can be directly equated with (re)action, and salvation (perfection) lies in moving into a state where non-action is possible. Thus the whole idea that 'man is born in sin' becomes a little less condemnatory and more descriptive of a state we can do something about. All we have to do to return to the Source is to achieve a state of cosmic balance; and an understanding of the cosmic mechanism will help us on the path to its realisation.

The simplistic view of sin as our lot because we live in a world based on reactive energy does not absolve us from all responsibility to try to be 'good'; all it does is to give us another viewpoint on what 'goodness' is. It is not sufficient to say that all our actions are inevitable results of previous conditions, and are therefore unavoidable; for then we become victims of fate, and are to be pitied for our incapacity to act according to conscience. Such an attitude circumvents our responsibility to try to return to a reaction-less state. 'What is the point?' ask the fatalists. 'All is preordained and dependent on what has gone before. We cannot change the course of the action/reaction process.' Such reasoning would appear to be logical, but it does not take two things into account.

Firstly, as has already been said, the main way of returning to the reaction-less state is by becoming more *aware*. Increased awareness is not simple notice of what is happening around us, and then storing the memories in the brain. It means becoming more aware of the 'interconnectedness' of all things, the timelessness of reality, and the Cosmos/life energy in everything and everyone. These three phenomena are the main constituents of the Lattice system. None of them are part of the action/reaction process; so by concentrating on them, our individual Lattice patterning gradually adjusts its vibrations towards the ultimate perfect balance. In practice, this means that we channel our energies towards becoming less judgmental, more compassionate, and less concerned with frantic planning for a secure future. This is the sort of thing that Christ was talking about in his famous

dictum 'Take no thought for the morrow.' (Matthew 6:25 et
seq). A better translation is 'Be ye not anxious for your life,
what ye shall eat, what ye shall drink, ...' Christ wanted us
to be aware of our situations and circumstances, and to
value our experiences at the time of their occurrence. He did
not want us to be always looking at what might or might not
happen in the future. Awareness is always concerned with
the Now because that is all that there really is.

The second way of moving towards the ideal reactionless
state is to realise that there are times in each life when an
individual's cosmic energies are suddenly in balance. At
these times it is possible to step off the karmic wheel. These
times are similar to those periods at the end of each swing of
the pendulum when dynamic energy is zero and, just for an
instant, only potential energy exists. As was said in chapter
4, these instants are 'out of time'. At these instants, a reactionless move is possible, and we should try to be in the correct state for them when they come about. This correct state
is achieved by being as close to a state of balance, or total
awareness, as is possible: thus, being neither elated nor
depressed; saintly nor sinful, active nor passive. In other
words, it is being in a state of contentment and desirelessness. It is a state of passive activity, or active passivity. It is
not a state to be desired, because desire will counteract the
necessity for desirelessness. It is a state to be entered
unknowingly — and the only way to arrive at that state is by
the constant practice of acceptance. This practice automatically reduces one's ability to 'sin' because acceptance generates the minimum of reactive processes. Acceptance is
achieved by meditation, prayer or attunement. In terms of
the energies of the Lattice, it is a slowing down of the lower
energies and an enrichment of the higher ones. These are
better able to resonate with the pure spiritual energy which
can take us across the boundary into the Source energy.

Divine punishment as an outside force imposed by a 'just
and merciful' god is another of humanity's puritanical ideas

devised to frighten wrongdoers into submission, thereby lessening tensions within the community. It is a distorted view of the karmic process. Rewards and punishments have always been regarded as a good way to control children and underlings. But this form of control is limited in that it does not work with intelligent victims, and it eventually loses its force even with the unintelligent ones. It also allows the self-righteous to congratulate themselves on their godliness in the same way that the Pharisees in the parables became super-smug. Unfortunately, this self-congratulatory process is almost as retrogressive as is wrongdoing. The middle way between being too saintly and too much of a sinner is very narrow indeed! The general guideline is that, if any self-gratification is involved at all — either as a feeling of pride, humiliation, despair or disgust — the middle way has been temporarily abandoned.

All our actions, whether physical, emotional or mental modify the energy vibrations of the Lattice strings, and these modified vibrations then become the patterns by which we live. If we create the same types of vibrations time and time again, the corresponding Lattice patterns will become very strong and will tend to attract other similar energies which will then vibrate sympathetically. Thus the miserable person attracts misery and the happy person attracts happiness. The person who expects accidents will find that accidents happen, and the person who expects miracles will live in a miraculous world. It should be understood at this point that the temperament which a person shows on the surface is not necessarily the same as the one which is actuating that person from inside. (In other words, we all have strong sub-personalities which can cause very strong emotional forces of which we are not consciously aware.) Thus, the apparently happy person may find himself or herself involved in many miserable situations because of a subconscious desire for punishment. Until these sub-personalities are brought to the surface and dealt with, their energy of attraction within the

Lattice will continue.

Many modern therapies, such as Gestalt, are designed to make us more aware of these underlying currents; but a simple examination of what appears to be going on itself can be a good guide as to our probable Lattice patterns. And once an honest appraisal has been made, balancing action can then be taken. Do I find that my best laid plans always seem to go awry? If so, I am likely to have a sub-conscious desire to be a 'victim', attracting pity as a substitute for lack of love. However, if I were to become more conscious of my surroundings and start to radiate my natural love towards other people and things, the Lattice energy will then change for the better and my series of disasters will stop. This will be easier said than done; but the process does get easier with practice.

We each have our own pendulum governing the pulse rate of our lives; and it will take thousands of attempts and the eventual help of a Master before we even begin to understand our own particular rhythm. But by feeling the vibrations in the Lattice around us, we can begin the journey on the road back to self-awareness and self-responsibility. Once the necessity of this important initial step is truly acknowledged, the vibrations in the nearby strings of the Lattice will automatically alter and the first step will become a reality. It is a fact constantly emphasised by many philosophies that we mirror our surroundings, and that everything we react to is a facet of our own nature. This is another way of saying that the vibrations of the Lattice within us continue outwards and influence or are influenced by our neighbourhood and what is occurring within it.

The eventual assistance of a Master is necessary to indicate those instants at which the end of our pendulumswings occur. We cannot recognise such states ourselves because desirelessness necessitates a total unawareness of self. A genuine Master, having already attained a state of cosmic awareness in which the rhythms of the Lattice can be recognised, will be able to sense the major rhythms in other people and guide them towards the right actions. The Master does not have to be physically present at any time: often all communications are sent at an intuitive level and direct physical contact is never made. Furthermore, as a person draws nearer to the balanced state by practising acceptance and desirelessness, so the pattern around that person in the Lattice becomes more obvious to those trained to see it, and the right helper will appear automatically. There is generally no need to go seeking help; it will come at the right time.

The times of zero pendulum movement are the times when the individual has the opportunity to act like the mythical phoenix and become reborn in the fire of Spirit. According to legend, the phoenix is a bird that lives for anything between 500 and 1,500 years and renews itself by building its own funeral pyre; then uttering an unearthly cry, it cremates itself upon it. Out of the ashes rises a new phoenix, more perfect and lovely than the last. Similarly, the human spirit has the ability to go back into spiritual energy, to be reborn again at a higher level.

Thus reincarnation and karma go hand in hand as the keys to the best way for each of us to follow our own particular paths. They also make good sense when contemplated from the scientific point of view. Reincarnation takes into account the universal rule that energy cannot be lost, but can only be transformed. As mentioned earlier, it doesn't matter whether the energy is physical, emotional, mental or spiritual; there is always the possibility of interchange between the types, and this is exactly what happens between incarnations. This is a difficult concept for western minds to accept, mainly because the religions of the past 2000 years have emphasised rewards and punishments as the way to deal with a congregation of saints and sinners. Religious morality has been based on a 'thou shalt not' policy, and reincarnation does not easily fit in this philosophy.

Likewise, karma is compatible with the scientific concept that action and reaction are equal and opposite. However, many western religions require a divine presence to act as a sort of ombudsman between each soul and God. Thus, the perfect balance inherent in the Karmic Law has been re-interpreted as something that can only be modified if you put a word in the right ear. This, once again, takes us back to the rewards and punishments system. In this way, religions such as Christianity have been able to control millions of people throughout the ages. This is not as important now as it used to be; but from about 400 AD until very recently, the Christian church effectively ruled the western world. The bishops, cardinals and the Pope were the people who controlled kings and nobles. They amassed great wealth, gloried in great power and were not always good spiritual examples to the people — the Borgias, for example. Thus religion has for many years been greatly influenced by politics. Reincarnation and karma are purely spiritual/scientific principles that do not need to be watered down or adapted to religio-political ends.

At this point in our investigation of life we have looked at Cosmos, the Lattice, time, space, energy, the soul, reincarnation, and karma. There are two main areas yet to explore. One is the way in which the Lattice energies are divided into special qualities and how those qualities interact— a continuation of polarisation — which we will examine in the next chapter.

Chapter 9

The Four Natural Elements

Up to this point, we have been discovering the basic constituents of our universe, and how a familiarity with them
can help to make our journey more delightful. With the
knowledge we have acquired, we are now better able to look
at the constituents of the two fundamental energies of the
Lattice, potential and dynamic, in greater detail. A clearer
understanding of how these energies work will be invalu-
able when we come to assess the various things that seem to
happen to us as we traverse our path. We will understand
the mysteries of magic and miracles more easily, and will be
less confused by what appear to be the quirks of fate which
cause us confusion and pain. At the same time, we will
increase our awareness of the pleasures there are along the
way.

We know that the Lattice gaps are filled with potential and
that this is the Source energy which feeds our dynamic universe. We also know that it is timeless, universal, and known
in religious terminology as God, (although we are calling it
Cosmos to reduce its religious colouring). We also know that
there are a large number of different types of dynamic energy, including physical, emotional, mental and spiritual. In
this chapter, we will concentrate on the way these active
energies divide into further types. These divisions will cate-
gorise the energies by their basic cosmic characteristics. This
will help us to see exactly how they interrelate and how we
can use them more efficiently. The basis of everything we
do, think, feel and desire is derived from these energies; so
the more we know about them, the more we will be able to
work with them, and understand why we react to situations
in the way that we do.

We are not going to delve deeply into motive — that is better left in the hands of psychologists and other specialists. Nor are we going to torture ourselves with self-analysis. That also is best left to specialists. What we *are* going to do is to look at the 'flavours' of the cosmic energy make-up. Some people prefer one flavour; some another. Preferences are dependent on what we each decided to do in this particular life. (Remember the purpose of reincarnation). So, by increasing our knowledge of the range of flavours, and by understanding our reactions to situations, we remember more clearly the movements we have decided to take along this particular part of the path. These are the aspects of our 'curriculum' which we have decided to concentrate on in this life.

One of the great teachers in the past who based much of his philosophy on a system known as 'the four elements' was Pythagoras. He had a maxim, of which the first half was also engraved over the entrance to the oracle at Delphi; it was: 'Man, know thyself, and hence thou shalt know God'. Pythagoras was trying to make his pupils understand that self-awareness is the key to the mysteries of life, and the way back to the Source. We are totally and exclusively composed of the energies of the four elements and Cosmos. When we fully understand how these elements act and interact, there will only be Cosmos left to become familiar with. Which is always our ultimate goal.

Although it is possible to travel to the Source along many routes, a relatively easy and comprehensible one for western minds is that of first acquiring a good working knowledge of the four elements. This will help to resolve the riddle of time, which is contained within this elemental knowledge. Time and logic are hopelessly mixed together. Eventually we need to move beyond logic to give intuition, and therefore Spirit, a chance of passing us clear and uncensored messages. But first of all, we need to use our strong logical capabilities to show us the way. Ultimately, we will reach the point where logic is superseded by intuition, and the time-lessness of reality becomes not just understood, but *realised*. An understanding of the four natural elements will aid this transition.

The categorisation of the elements we are going to use is based on a philosophy which has been known for many thousands of years. It was used by the ancient Egyptians and later by the great Greek teachers during the 500 years before Christ. Then, later still, it was used by the alchemists of the middle ages. The philosophy basically says that every-thing in the universe is composed of a mixture of just four energies, called the 'natural' Elements: FIRE, WATER, AIR and EARTH. There are no other elements, and no other ener-gies in the universe, apart from Cosmos). Absolutely every-thing else without exception is made of just these four.

It is important to understand right from the start that these natural elements are not the same as their physical counterparts; neither are they the elements in the accepted chemical sense. They have names which are the same as four common chemical combinations because they can be identi-fied with them in many ways, but they should not be mis-taken for each other. The use of the names of everyday sub-stances was an *aide memoire* suggested by the ancients so that the primary qualities of these energy divisions could be more easily learned. They are called 'elements' because they are the primary ingredients of the universe, in the same way that the chemical elements form the basic 'stuff' of physical life. In the following text, they will always be written in cap-itals to distinguish them from their everyday equivalents.

Keeping in mind the Lattice, these natural elements are the four basic resonances of the energies in the Lattice strings. They can be compared loosely to the four sections of an orchestra: brass, strings, woodwind, and percussion. Just as an orchestra includes many variations within these four sections, (and many unrelated modern instruments besides — a metal flute is classed as a woodwind), so the natural

Elements cause a variety of resonances in the Lattice, some of which seem similarly to have moved a long way from their original classifications. However, just as a metal flute makes a sound very similar to a wooden one, so the variations within each Elemental category are basically similar to its originating energy.

We will look at the Elements in the order they appear out of the cosmic energy of potential. As everything derives originally from that Source, so the four Elements emerge as a series, starting with FIRE.

The Elemental FIRE

Ordinary fire in its natural state is undirected energy: it is uncontrolled energy which moves in all directions at once rather than one specific way. If the temperature is sufficiently high, everything will burn including glass and metal. These are also the basic characteristics of FIRE — it is totally uncontrolled; it cannot be said to favour any particular direction or thing; and it is capable of giving life to all things. Just like Spirit and just like life, it will move into anything that gives it a chance.

The adjective 'untamed' is sometimes associated with a large fire — such as a bush fire which is out of control. Similarly, the elemental FIRE is the emergent untamed primary cosmic energy. Just like ordinary fire, it has great power and can be difficult to control. The type of natural fire with which FIRE is best compared is the raw output from an erupting volcano, a wild energy going up, out, and down at the same time.

FIRE is the basic life in all things, whether they be animal, vegetable, mineral, emotional, mental, or spiritual. It is the driving force which activates the whole of creation; and without its presence, all vitality in our perceived world would grow cold and cease to exist. All created things must contain a proportion of FIRE, however small. It is the essential dynamic energy which transforms potential into what we see as the world about us. Mountains and mole-hills contain this energy of life just as much as animals and apples. If the energy of FIRE is absent at a nodal point in the Lattice, no other energies can be transformed at that point, and the node is effectively inert. Absence of FIRE means absence of existence. The life-force of FIRE is the miracle seen by the cosmic burglar alarm at the instant that time started and it first observed the 'intruder'. (see chapter 4.)

At this point, it is worthwhile diverting for a paragraph or two in order to look at the ancient Greek legend of Prometheus, who first brought the fire of the gods to humanity. Although there is a lot which is obviously untrue in these myths, once we look below the surface we will usually find that they contain a great deal of wisdom and basic truth about the universe. This particular legend demonstrates the penalty inherent in misusing the energy of FIRE, as well as its essential power.

Prometheus and his brother, Epimetheus, were two of the sons of the Titan Eurymedon. (The Titans were the all-powerful divine giants, fore-runners of the Olympian Gods.) They were persuaded by Zeus, the ambitious and amoral head of the gods of Olympus, to forsake their kin and help the gods to overcome and enslave the other Titans and the great god, Cronus. (Cronus was the grandfather of Zeus and the father of Uranus). But after the war was won with the help of the brothers, Zeus, instead of being eternally grateful to them for their help, became extremely angry with Prometheus, who had observed during the battles just how hard the lot of humanity was — at that time not much better than that of the animals — and had decided to give mankind some sort of help. Zeus, on the other hand, felt that the species was too corrupt and not worth saving; so he was all for its total destruction. Prometheus, however, was convinced that the basic trouble with human beings was that they had never been given a real chance to prove their worth, so he stole some of the sacred fire of the Gods in a fennel stalk, smuggling it out of Olympus to give to them. This fire would enable them to cook their meat, keep warm at night, and forge tools from base metals, thereby becoming more than simple hunting animals on two legs.

Zeus had found out what had happened while his back was turned and he was so incensed that he caught Prometheus, chained him to a rock and sentenced him to having his liver continually pecked by a vulture. (At night his liver would grow again so that there would be more for the vulture to peck at the next day!) Epimetheus, seeing the terrible wrath of Zeus, (who was definitely a rather dictatorial and unpredictable God), decided that discretion could be the better part of valour. Hoping that Zeus would look more kindly on his own kith and kin, he quickly married a close relation of Zeus, Pandora.

After the hurried wedding, he moved into his new home with his bride, taking with him a special box that Prometheus had given him for safe keeping and never to be opened. Pandora, who was as inquisitive as she was beautiful, found the box one day and opened it. Out flew all the Spites which Prometheus had been careful to keep locked away from humanity. Thus Old Age, Sickness, Vice, Insanity, Passion, and Labour were let loose to trouble the world. Thankfully, Hope came out of the box at the same time in order to save humanity from mass suicide.

The legend can be interpreted at many levels, as all good legends can. For example, a translation of the names of the main characters is instructive. Prometheus means 'forethought; Epimetheus means 'afterthought'; Cronus means 'time'; and Pandora means 'all-giving'. The interpretation of these aspects of the story is left for your own amusement.

The truth behind this particular legend possibly relates to the Atlantean period and an earlier discovery of atomic power which perchance led to the near annihilation of our world. The fire taken from the Gods could have been atomic power itself, given to a morally immature humanity by a well-meaning but myopic scientist. Zeus's anger could have been the accidental or malicious release of multi-megaton atomic bombs. The marriage of Epimetheus could have been an attempt to make good the tremendous harm done. And the release of the Spites could have been the inevitable outcome of such a dismal set of circumstances. Or it may simply have been a cautionary tale from wise people of old: that powerful forces must not be given out thoughtlessly because both bad as well as good consequences can be the result. Whatever the meaning of the fine print, it is interesting to note that time (Cronus) was acknowledged by the wise old Greeks as the original forbear of the other energies of the universe (represented in their stories by the gods), and that FIRE was seen to be the most essential energy for progress.

Whether Atlantis ever existed and whether an atomic catastrophe caused its destruction is unimportant as far as our present interpretation of the legend is concerned. It is mentioned to show that there are other ways of looking at causes and effects apart from the ones given here. What is important to our present discussion is that FIRE energy can cause such a calamity, and yet it is also an essential part of the make-up of the universe. It is the primary cosmic energy, from which all the others are derived. It can be effectively considered the highest cosmic 'voltage', and may be compared to the high voltage distribution network channelling power from generating stations to different parts of the country. Unless this very high voltage is properly insulated and treated with great respect, it can literally vapourise the unwary. On the other hand, used wisely and with proper respect, it brings enormous benefits to the peoples of the land.

As far as the majority of civilised countries are concerned, electricity may be considered as the stuff of life itself, and FIRE its elemental equivalent. FIRE is the prime energy from which all life as we know it emerges. This point cannot be stressed too much — that *all* of creation contains life, not just animals and vegetables. It is not possible to imagine anything which is not basically alive. The rhythms of life-forms vary enormously from each other: from the extremely high-speed life energy of electromagnetism, through to the middle-speed life energy of human beings, down to the very slow-speed life energy of mountains and suchlike. In all cases, the FIRE energy is resonating at the nodal points of the Lattice, thereby creating the patterns of what we sense as 'things'.

Esoteric writings teach that Masters can channel the power of FIRE energy using the solar plexus into a focussed force either to create or destroy other life forms. The correct term, however is 'change': the change of one life form to another; because we now know that energy can neither be created nor destroyed. This is similar to the teachings of such disciplines as T'ai Chi, which state that the storage place for Chi, or life force, is at the solar plexus chakra. 'Solar plexus' is Latin for the 'lattice point of the sun:' this particular area of the human body is where a predominance of the FIRE nodes are situated. Misuse of FIRE energy can cause anything from stomach ache to chronic cancer of the stomach. 'Misuse' occurs when this powerful energy is incorrectly focussed, and some of it 'leaks' backwards, thereby upsetting the physical body, from which it originates. The amount of leakage will determine the severity of the subsequent illness. Incorrect focussing is generally the result of insufficient preparation or impure motives.

So, to recapitulate, FIRE is the primary cosmic energy coming from the Source. It is an undirected energy of immense power which gives birth to all aspects of life. As it is of no use to us in this untamed state, we need a 'controller' for it — WATER.

The Elemental WATER

WATER is the element of polarisation and separation; and yet it is also the element which demonstrates unity by balance. It is like ordinary water because it is always trying to achieve balance — for water is always trying to find a common level. It is also like the sea in that a placid surface can hide strong undercurrents, while a stormy surface can conceal calm waters. It is an element of contradictions because of the opposing forces it contains. Separation versus unity; tumult versus calmness; chaos versus control. Like the pendulum we discussed in chapter 3, the balance contained within WATER is a dynamic balance which is always oscillating between its limits. It demonstrates that true balance, in contrast to non-moving potential, is a continually changing state. A pendulum is no longer useful if it stops swinging; and life is no longer progressive if it loses its differences. The primary energy of FIRE requires the polarising energy of WATER to direct it into useful channels. Thus, WATER energy is derived from the FIRE energy, but it directs that energy into lower energy patterns which are usable. FIRE cannot be used properly without WATER; and WATER cannot be brought into existence except by FIRE.

WATER is also a part of the energy behind emotion. The human psyche has a great desire to bathe in the effervescence of this emotional energy. WATER energy gives the psyche great power and a sense of purpose. The effervescence is at its most scintillating when these opposites are knocking sparks out of each other. The clue to using this energy positively is not the total suppression of the emotional forces leading to the reduction of the flow to a trickle, but the proper channelling of the energy into carefully constructed irrigation lines which feed the WATER sparingly to every part of the human system without letting it become stagnant.

Stagnation occurs when the energy is left too long in any

one place, generating greed, hate, envy, malice, and all the other vices. It also occurs, surprisingly enough, if excessive emotional love is present. Most forms of human love are possessive in origin, and can be traced back to a need for security. Security-consciousness is a form of anti-activity which tries to negate the risk factor inherent in cosmic progress by damping down the FIRE. Anything which acts to *reduce* the energy of FIRE rather than to *direct* it is part of the stagnation process.

In its purest form, love is a unifying energy, the cosmic driving force behind WATER. It is Buddhic by nature. This type of love is very difficult to comprehend because it is on a much higher plane than its shadowy cousin, possessive love. Part of WATER's unification energy lies in the realisation that separation is an illusion, for all things are interconnected. As the elemental energies move away from the Source, we find that this basic cosmic fact seems to become more of a vague memory than a reality. However, it remains part of the underlying cosmic make-up of each one of us. One of the hardest demonstrations of pure love is the ability to let go of that which we love — to become separated from it. This separation is an illusion at cosmic levels, although it appears very real at the physical level. So WATER also contains the energy of illusion.

WATER energy is full of enigmas: whatever it appears to be in one instant, it is the opposite an instant later. A clue to resolving this difficulty is to realise that opposites are only opposite because they contain the potential to be each other. For instance, 'high' is opposite to 'low', but not to 'left' or to 'right'. 'High' and 'low' are opposites because they both measure vertical space.Therefore they are related. They are held together by the invisible string of perpendicularity. Similarly 'good' and' bad' are held together by the string of morality. All opposites must have these strings in order to be opposite. The strings are very long; so that what is good at one moment can become bad at the next, depending on where the centre of the string is chosen. Taoism expresses this delightfully in the *Tao Tê Ching* where it says:

> *When all the world understand beauty to be*
> *beautiful, then ugliness exists.*
> *When all understand goodness to be good,*
> *then evil exists.*
> . . . .
> *Short is derived from long by comparison;*
> *Low is distinguished from high by position;*
> *Resonance harmonises sound;*
> *After follows before.*

The verse above, which was written a couple of thousand years before Einstein, points out that all things are relative. Thus, depending on one's point of view, 'high' becomes 'low', 'good' becomes 'bad', etc. All this comes from the energy of WATER. WATER is necessary to control FIRE; and all the opposites and the difficulties it brings with it comes from this need for control. It is well worth remembering that in order to be happy we must accept the possibility of misery. In order to be satisfied we must accept the possibility of insufficiency. In order to be good we must accept our capacity for evil. It is not possible to exist in our world only at one end of the pendulum's swing. This is one of the lessons of Pandora's box, that the gods never encumber humanity with only one aspect of an energy. There is always the opposite lurking about somewhere. In other words, the Law of Karma is always with us, making available the opportunity for balance.

WATER is also the driving force behind instinct and intuition. Intuition is one of our direct links with Cosmos, via the energy of FIRE (Spirit). All creation has a continuous stream of messages passing along to it on the Lattice strings via cosmic spirit. Unfortunately for humankind, those messages are mostly ignored, misunderstood, or lost because of all the other information we receive at the same time via the five normal senses. This sensual information is considered by us as being more important and reliable than these messages because it has been filtered by the intellect, which is nearer to our logical processes. Logic, thought and emotions — the constituents of the personality triangle described in chapter 6 — are the ultimate realities as far as we are concerned.

The judgmental nature of WATER energy is frequently over-accentuated; and its vibrations tend to so swamp the FIRE energy that intellect is admired and intuition is ridiculed. This is one of the prices we pay for living in a logic-oriented society. As in all things, the ideal is a proper balance between the two. WATER, like its natural counterpart, will find a common level if it is given a chance. But it is susceptible to turbulence and, once disturbed, can take a long time to become placid again. Beneath its apparently tranquil surface, the emotions and instincts which it engenders may be creating all kinds of contrary currents. These powerful forces should be used to help us on our journey, but, in practice, they tend to take over and govern our existence. The reasons for this will be discussed shortly in the chapter on the Devic kingdom.

The Elemental AIR

In human terms, AIR is equated with the mental plane, and is therefore very powerful, particularly in the western world where logic rules supreme. The simile of gaseous air is used for this element because of its transient nature, and also because it can be a powerful yet unseen force. We must be careful not to confuse the mental energy of this Element with the intuitive energy WATER. Intuition and instinct often manifest themselves as 'nous' (pronounced 'nowss') — the natural ability to take the right course of action in unfamiliar situations. Nous is sometimes confused with intellect, although they are very dissimilar. A totally uneducated person can have lots of nous but be quite incapable of answering a standard intelligence test because he does not have the vocabulary or knowledge to do so. But he will still have natural instincts and an understanding of the way the world operates. One of the weaknesses of many intelligence tests is that they require intellect in order to answer the questions. Nous and intellect are both forms of intelligence, with the difference that nous is an understanding of the ways of the natural world while intellect is a knowledge of the ways of our constructed environment. It can be said that nous is WATER with a bit of AIR in it, while intellect is mainly AIR on its own.

Note also that AIR, being derived from FIRE via WATER, contains the qualities of the latter two. This means that all mental images contain life and are therefore capable, to some extent, of an independent existence. This is an important point to remember, as it shows that it is both possible to leave after-effects from strong thought patterns as well as to affect events at the time of thinking. The effects will generally be very small; but in times of great emotional stress, the amount of FIRE energy passed into the mental realm can be quite large, resulting in thoughts so powerful that they can literally make or break a particular outcome. (This is discussed further in chapters 11 and 12.)

The natural forces with which the cosmic energies are compared were chosen very carefully to give a guide to the characteristics of their elemental counterparts.The comparisons cannot be perfect because the Elements are so much more than can be explained or demonstrated by any one phenomenon. However, the *flavour* of the Element can be gleaned by examination of the corresponding earthly equivalent. Thus, the partial control of AIR may be seen by examining how natural air can be channelled to benefit us all. For instance, if the wind is blowing strongly, a building might be flattened by the storm, because it could not flex against the moving air. But if the structure is correctly designed, the wind's power can then be harnessed positively and, for instance, operate a windmill or drive a ship. In both instances, the wind is not directly opposed, but is carefully diverted instead. The sails of a windmill direct the wind, taking *some* of its energy for their own diversion into a circle of force. Similarly, the sails of a ship are set to use the wind's movement towards the progress of the ship across the water, even while the wind is blowing directly against the direction in which the ship wants to go. The principle of tacking into the wind is an important part of this simile, as it shows that even when AIR energy appears to be in direct conflict with one's path, a series of 'tacks' will allow progress to be made in the desired direction.

It is generally the fear of pain or ridicule that makes us stiffen into unyielding buildings instead of relaxing into sails. This self-induced stiffness causes exactly the opposite result from what we want to achieve and gives the AIR a solid surface to destroy. By listening to the intuitive WATER messages given to us all the time however, we should be able to understand that all cosmic energies are basically beneficial. Relaxed public speakers can use the destructive energies of the barracker to turn the tables, and a good debater will use the arguments of the opposition to enhance his or her own case. A good balance between WATER and AIR is the best way forward. This is where people with nous have a better chance of survival in adverse circumstances than do people possessing solely intellect. (For instance, nous will tell you which unfamiliar foods are poisonous; intellect won't. Watch the way in which wild animals avoid the things that are bad for them.)

This leads us on to the energy of instinct, which is mainly a WATER energy, with a small amount of AIR energy attached. It is not purely WATER, as is intuition, because it is an inherited trait. All inherited characteristics are composed mainly of AIR and EARTH, because they compose the personality of human beings. (Remember the section in chapter 6 which discussed the lower manas of the soul and how that is the main part which reincarnates.) Although reincarnation and inheritance are not the same thing, as part of the process of deciding which energies will be best for the next life, the soul chooses suitable parents and the appropriate instinctual energy is then passed on by them. Thus the reincarnation process indirectly determines inheritance.

The Elemental EARTH

EARTH is the last of the four basic energies of the cosmic scheme, and it gives stability to the higher life forces. It gives physical substance to these other energies and represents final results. Just as the Earth is a place where we can build a home and feel safe, so EARTH represents the energy of security. The security and stability it gives can act together as a temporary resting place while the lessons learned during the journey are being assimilated; or conversely, they can be used as an excuse for stagnation. That is its main danger. The journey to the discovery of Self is not easy, and it is tempting to want to rest 'just a little longer', but if the pause is too long, the spiritual muscles will begin to go soft, making the next part of the journey even more difficult. The quiet and insistent voice of the human mind tells us that there is no such thing as the Path, and that all this striving is sheer masochism, so why not stretch out and enjoy the luxuries that EARTH can offer? But behind that soft persuasive voice, there is another voice to be heard; the WATER voice of intuition. Deep, deep down we each *know* that there is more to life than lazing around at the resting place, so it is better to take short rests and then to move on before the spiritual muscles become stiff. The previous lessons, stored in the higher mind, will always tell us the correct direction to take in order to continue our journey.

As far as the human body is concerned, EARTH energy is

stored in the physical and astral bodies, the latter of which contains the emotions. These are the *lower* emotions, sometimes called the adrenaline emotions, as opposed to the *higher*, or aesthetic emotions, which are part of the higher manas and reside in the higher mind. The lower emotions protect the body, and are all based on fear: fear of attack; fear of starvation; fear of not propagating the species; fear of extinction of the tribe. Thus terror facilitates the body's flow of adrenaline in order to give it a sudden boost of energy when escaping from hazardous situations; and greed encourages the body to take in large quantities of nourishment in case there is a famine just round the corner; and envy produces extra strength in the envier in order to overcome an adversary and then take his possessions — food, shelter, a mate, etc; and hate calls up energy reserves in order to fight and win; and so on.

The raw instinct to survive does not exist to the same extent in the civilised world as it did in prehistoric times. Currently, it exists in Third World countries, as well as in the psyche of people such as drug addicts, because their bodies tell them that more drugs are essential in order to survive. Thus, drug addicts will steal, kill, or maim in order to get their fix.

There are also what appear at first sight to be 'non-adrenaline' emotions such as misery, sorrow and despair. These emotions represent the fear within, which did not exist in humanity's original make-up. In prehistoric times, if a woman's mate was killed, her grief would increase her flow of adrenaline and help her to determine a way for her and her children to survive. As centuries went by, however and the basic 'you-either-live-or-you-die' type of existence diminished, the requirement for adrenaline at times of loss also diminished. But the reaction to loss is still a part of the human make-up. So it has gradually become turned inwards. In the extreme, it causes depression. This is the ultimate stagnation of adrenaline energy, and the only way out of it is to generate a good dose of fear or hate to get the adrenaline flowing again. It is interesting to note that in some societies, for example the Irish, a funeral is followed first by mourning and then by an energetic dance. This successfully counteracts the inward moving energies by burning them off in physical activity.

Thus the EARTH energy of the human being is a complex system which has changed greatly over the centuries. However, its basic function is still to provide a vehicle for the higher energies. This applies at every level. The AIR energies transmit experiences higher up the chain, and at the same time monitor the EARTHy part of the being in order to keep it in good shape. The WATER energy acts as a link between Spirit and matter, passing upwards the essence of human experiences and downwards the will and ability to live. The FIRE energy gives life to the whole system.

Until the beginnings of modern medicine, the four elements were closely associated with the human body as the four 'humours'. These were called blood, choler, phlegm, and black bile. In a healthy body, they would be in balance, and illness was considered to be caused by a predominance of one or more of the four. A fit person was judged to be 'in good humour', while unbalance caused a person to be in 'ill humour', and becoming sanguine, choleric, phlegmatic or bilious. Only these descriptions of human conditions now remain; diagnosis by humours having been replaced in the past 150 years by other forms of medical artistry. Perhaps categorisation of illness by humours was too simplistic — especially when we consider the complexities of drug technology — but it is still useful when assessing a person's mood.

When considering one's journey from the outside, the whole business of travelling back to the Source seems to be a desire to punish oneself, and no pleasure can be gleaned from it. It is rather like watching a white-water race. Can the participants *really* derive any pleasure from subjecting themselves to such danger and hardship? But we know that they do, because there is no necessity to take up the challenge in the first place. In the case of our individual journey however, there *is* a compulsion to take it because it is the only way down the river, and the goal is at the end past the rapids and the whirlpools. One might wait for the cosmic helicopter, but it will never come; the only way home is by literally taking the plunge.

Watching white-water contestants will show that the best way is not necessarily through the apparently calmer waters, but often through the most turbulent swirls. The short periods of rest are used simply to assess the patterns of the water in the next stage, and to regain some breath before plunging into the next part of the battle. Without the occasional short stretch of relative calm, it is probable that most of the participants would drown; and this is equally true of the periods of rest afforded us by EARTH.

The whole cosmic system is perfect in its simplicity. The four energies provide activity, challenge, achievement, and rest. They provide the sum total of what is necessary for progress of any sort. Without activity there could be no start at all; without challenge there would be no clear direction in which to move; without achievement there would be no way of measuring the progress made; and without rest there would be no time to assimilate the purpose of the exercise. So EARTH, although a passive energy, is equally as important as FIRE. No complete system can operate efficiently without both stimulus and appreciation.

Within EARTH are held the energies of the other three elements. It is the most stable of the four. However, it can be very difficult to re-establish the status quo if unbalance is generated within it. Consider the balance between FIRE and AIR within EARTH. As it is the element which governs material possessions, a lot of activity (FIRE) once put into the accumulation (AIR) of possessions will form a very rigid pattern, thereby causing the unbalanced characteristics of miserliness, bigotry or ruthlessness to take hold. Likewise, if a lot of energy is put into challenge (WATER), the other half of EARTH, which is also WATER, will then cause total polarisation to take place so that no decisions can be made at all! It can be very difficult to get past the states of inertia or rigidity which are both present in EARTH. So the all-abiding rule to guide the traveller along the way still applies: balance and contentment in all things.

COSMOS   POTENTIAL

ENERGY BARRIER

FIRE	Spirit, Life energy
WATER	Polarisation, intuition, desire
AIR	Creativity, time, mind
EARTH	Stability, physical, emotional

TABLE OF COSMOS AND THE ELEMENTS

The four Elements have been a part of spiritual teachings from prehistory. It is interesting to compare the description of the Creation, as set down in the Old Testament with the emergence of the four elements described above. The beginning of Genesis says that on the first day God divided the light from the darkness, which is comparable with the emergence of FIRE from Zero. (As Zero does not exist in the realised universe, it must be the ultimate darkness). On the second day, He divided the firmament from the waters and called it heaven. This is analogous to the creation of WATER and AIR. Then, on the third day He created dry land (EARTH). Having produced these four basic elemental energies, He then went on to produce animal and human life forms before using the energy of EARTH for a well-earned rest Himself.

There are many similar accounts in ancient writings which contain clues as to the secrets of the creative process. Reading the Greek, Norse, or Indian myths can be both an informative exercise and a relaxing pastime.

In the next chapter we will see how the Elements become other entities specially programmed to channel their energies to the different life patterns on Earth.

Chapter 10

Angels and Fairies

Having looked at the way the Lattice and humanity interplay with each other and Cosmos, it is now time to look at some of the non-human and 'unseen' forces and their role in the universe. By unseen forces we mean those with a special duty to help the other life forms of the universe, rather than phenomena like electromagnetism and gravity. These special forces appear to have intelligence and to be self-actuating but we will see during this chapter that they are actually 'programmed' rather like computers. Although computers often appear to have free-will, they are actually totally reliant on the instructions they have been given, and are not capable of independent decisions.

We are now going to look at the major source of these unseen forces — the Devic Kingdom. The main inhabitants of this kingdom are what are broadly called angels, demons and fairies. The mention of such entities may cause your eyebrows to rise and summon the sceptic in you. However, please try to keep an open mind and see whether you are still sceptical by the end of this chapter.

The mention of entities such as angels and fairies is very frequently met with scepticism in the western world. However, until the Industrial Revolution, our belief systems were different and most ordinary people either 'believed' in fairies or at least did not consider believers to be mad. But such convictions are now considered totally unacceptable unless you are eccentric. This is unfortunate because these entities continually interact with humanity to keep this world of ours running. There would be far less pollution and better uses of our natural resources if more people acknowledged and co-operated with this unseen side of nature.

Although most major religions express belief in angelic and demonic forces, few people in our modern and materialistic world take the implications of such belief seriously. Christians sing carols at Christmas about shepherds being visited by angels; they read about an angel guarding the tomb after Christ's crucifixion; and they read about Christ casting out devils and transferring them into a herd of swine. The Moslem faith requires a belief in the Angel of God, and also believes that the Koran was dictated to Mohammed by the angel Gabriel. There are many mentions of angels bringing messages from God in the writings of Judaism, and Zoroastrian writings include references to guardian angels. But if the average person who professes a belief in God is asked if he or she also believes in the presence of angels in everyday life, the answer would probably be an emphatic *no*. The general opinion is that if angels should by some remote chance happen to exist, then they should do the decent thing and save their activities for recognised religious festivals.

It is particularly difficult for modern scientists, who need a rational explanation for everything, to accept that there are forces in existence which do not necessarily behave according to scientific formulae. That scepticism has now spilled over into the lives of the ordinary community, replacing the older beliefs nurtured by the early Christian Church. This is a shame because, as has already been pointed out, a belief in angels can add a whole new dimension to life; it can also provide believers with much needed security. Furthermore, personal angels cost nothing to keep, are clean about the house, and do not need to be taken for walks! And contrary to popular belief, they do not spend their time watching out for misdemeanours so that they can earn Brownie points by reporting back to 'HIM upstairs'.

It is, of course, possible that the early leaders of world religions were all wrong; well-loved and long-cherished ideas have been found to be wrong in the past, so this one concerning angels, demons, and so forth may equally be proved wrong. But let's give it a chance first before throwing it onto the rubbish heap of tried and rejected notions. Hopefully, with our fresh view of the universe as a place governed by cosmic energies and interconnected by a timeless and limitless Lattice, there will be a place for the devic kingdom of angels, demons, fairies, and others. I say hopefully because these particular entities can serve a very useful purpose in this new scheme of things.

Habit is a strong taskmaster, and the habit of holding onto beliefs and disbeliefs is one of the strongest that we have. Generally, habits are based upon insecurity and fear of the unknown. We continue to hold on to our strong opinions because we are frightened to risk a change to something new. 'Better the devil we know, etc.' (Whoops! that's one of the devic kingdom creeping in already; devils are part of that scheme of things). But risk is often the best way forward, and unless we occasionally break with habits and tradition we will make very slow and boring progress. Nowhere in this book will you be asked to accept anything as absolutely true for all time: all the ideas expressed are put forward as *possibilities* which may be helpful. As long as human beings continue to be progressive thinking machines (even if very complex ones), ideas will go on being replaced by other ideas, including the ones expressed here.

Angels, demons, fairies, and others, are all part of the devic kingdom of the universe. The word 'kingdom' is used simply as an all-embracing collective noun; it is not meant to imply that there is an actual king ruling over these entities. Devic is the adjective derived from the Sanskrit Deva, meaning 'shining one'. This kingdom includes archangels, angels, gnomes, fairies, naiads, undines, genii, imps, devils, demons, archdemons and elementals. All these entities have work to do in helping to channel the energies of the Lattice with what we can generally call 'nature energy'. Remember that there are very many different types of vibration, and that the electromagnetic spectrum is only a tiny part of the whole system. Each different type of vibration helps or hinders other types, but cannot necessarily be captured or recognised by instruments which are designed to observe only a small part of the overall cosmic spectrum. Thus, devic energy is useful in communicating information from one part of the Lattice to another, but the actual information transfer mechanism may be transparent to our normal scientific measuring apparatus. It is a bit like trying to measure sound waves with an electric meter, or taste with a thermometer — measuring instruments are designed with a particular response in mind and will not register to the wrong stimuli. At the moment, apart from animal and vegetable sensitivity, there has been no equipment designed which reliably responds to the subtle energies of the devic kingdom.

One of the reasons why the average person finds it difficult to accept the possibility that these devic beings exist is because they have been endowed with human shape by fairy stories and legends. Thus, they are subconsciously taken to be superhuman and are generally expected to share human likes and dislikes in the same way as the gods of mythology. As we humans cannot fly unaided or become invisible we have a natural antipathy to other beings in apparent human form who are able to do these things, and we therefore tend to deny their existence. Imagine what it would be like if subatomic particles had originally been described as being of human form. Little electrons with wings joining hands with other little flying electrons to dance around groups of scowling neutrons and big fat positrons sitting about in groups. It is doubtful if atomic science would have become acceptable at all!

In reality, the devic energies, like atomic forces, have *no* fixed form. And they have no emotions and no free-will. They are simply centres of energy generated in the Lattice by a range of vibrations which is different from the electrodynamic spectrum. They almost always specialise in specific parts of the cosmic spectrum and are associated with one or other of the four Elements. Therefore they can be categorised as EARTH elementals, AIR elementals, etc. They have no visible support, (so they appear to 'fly'), they are non-physical, (so they are unaffected by gravity), and they cannot normally be seen or heard as their existential energy patterns are outside the range of vibrations to which the five common human senses are sensitive.

In some circumstances, they interact with parts of the normal physical spectrum and become visible or otherwise tangible to the sensory mechanisms of specially gifted humans, as visible forms, as sounds, or, occasionally, as transferred thoughts or feelings. As a general guide, it is best to imagine both angels and demons as simple centres of bright lights in different colours. (Hence the reference to 'shining ones'). But there are definitely no wings, no halos, and no pitchforks.

The same goes for goblins, elves, fairies, etc. They are all different types of elemental energy in small concentrated patterns which act as transformers and carriers for some of the basic cosmic energies within the Lattice. Angels are the elemental forces that perform the tasks we judge to be 'good', while demons are the forces that perform the tasks we deem 'bad'. The same judgmental categorisation goes for all the devic entities in the range between angels and elementals: fairies are generally 'good', goblins are generally 'bad', elves are 'good but a bit naughty', imps are 'bad', and so forth. In reality, of course, none of these forces is either good or bad, any more than electrons, neutrons, etc., can be termed good or bad. (Are the atoms disintegrating in the explosion of the atomic bomb 'bad' atoms and those which give us electricity from nuclear reactors 'good' atoms?). Of course not — they are simply aspects of the polarised cosmic energies which are doing the jobs they are programmed to do. In fact, the word angel comes from the Greek for messenger, and the word demon is a shortening of the original Greek daemon, meaning 'supernatural being'. So neither word has either good or bad categorisation. Angels are simply energy carriers and demons are other beings working outside the normal physical spectrum. It has only been in comparatively recent times that these two types of energy have been moved from their neutral categories and given human attributes.

All forms of devic energy are able to communicate with the human kingdom, though not by speech. (Being non-material energy patterns they have no vocal chords or larynx). They are, however, able to use telepathic communication. Telepathy uses vibrations along the Lattice strings which are within the same part of the cosmic spectrum as the fundamental devic energies. Basically, telepathic communication works by using picture language, not words. It is part of the AIR energy, but, where ordinary speech uses physical air for its transmission, telepathic messages use the Elemental AIR as medium instead. (Telepathic messages can travel much faster than light as they are not restricted to the speed of electromagnetic transmissions).

Most forms of elemental energy do not understand the logical sequence of ordinary speech. They simply transmit ideas and feelings. So a human recipient who happens to be, say, gardening may find that he or she is drawn to mulching one particular plant or pruning another, for no particular reason that he or she can think of. Some particularly sensitive people have achieved spectacular results when communicating in this way with EARTH elementals, as the books *The Magic of Findhorn* by Paul Hawken and *Behaving As If The God In All Life Really Mattered* by Machaelle Small Wright bear witness. These books demonstrate that proper communication with 'Nature Spirits', (or EARTH elementals), can improve the quantity and quality of plant life enormously. In the first case, Dorothy Maclean received messages from the elementals during her meditations concerning the correct methods for growing vegetables plus a few flowers and shrubs. In the second case, Machaelle Small Wright expanded the technique to include a method for asking the elementals whether particular gardening techniques are appropriate in specific places or at specific times.

When conversing with the elementals, the most reliable results are achieved by visualisation techniques, because these bypass the logic centres in the brain and are therefore less prone to judgmental censorship. Think of what you want to transmit as a *positive* picture: a picture of the required result rather than a negation of what you don't want. The lower forms of elementals do not understand the idea of 'not' so, if you would like it to stop raining for example, transmission of the idea that it will shortly *not* be raining will probably result in lots more rain. What is always required is a positive image of a sunny day, or dry ground, or clouds dispersing. Any thoughts which allow the idea of rain to be in the message will be interpreted as just that — rain —and the elementals will oblige and give you the rain that they sensed in your request. This 'don't think negative' technique is more difficult than it seems and requires a lot of practice. The human mind is a tricky thing and is not easy to control, so it is easy for little thoughts of rain to creep in round the corners of the visualisation of a sunny day. This is why so few of us are really successful telepathists or rain dispersers.

In order to understand more fully the type of forces we are dealing with in the devic kingdom, the various levels of energies will now be described, starting with the basic form — the elementals — and finishing with the most complex form — the archangels.

The four elementals.

The simplest form of devic life is that of the elementals. These are the 'worker bees' of the devic community and are generally responsible for putting the correct natural forces in the right place at the right time. They are not capable of making any decisions but act rather like programmed robots. If they appear to act in an independent manner, it will be a result of either inadequate programming or built-in instinctual behaviour patterns. Their activities are very close to the basic vibrations of Lattice energy and the life patterns they produce are generally of a very simple form.

There are elementals of all four primary cosmic energies. The FIRE elementals are very quick and diaphanous — like very hot flames, but without any heat of their own. They are best imagined as a thin veil of energy, constantly moving like a gauze curtain in a breeze. They are never found in isolation but always as a nebulous group and are always on the move. The philosopher Paracelsis, a 16th century Austrian alchemist, gave them the name 'salamanders'. The basic energy of life can easily be seen pulsating in the veil they form, like myriads of tiny dotted lights. (This was the experience of some of the experimenters with LSD in the 1960s.) The overall effect is a shining cloud of energy, generally almost colourless, like the shimmering air which can be seen reflected above a road surface on a hot summer's day.

(This shimmering is much the same as that described in chapter 4. Few people can see these manifestations if they look directly at them, but they can sometimes be seen out of the corner of one's eye. Peripheral vision contains better optical sensors for these diaphanous energies.)

Everyone and everything contains this continuous scintillation, because everyone and everything contains the basic FIRE energy of life. In human beings, it can be seen by psychically attuned people particularly in the astral body. At the time of a human being's death, this FIRE energy shimmer does not immediately vanish, but takes on a different glow and a different rate of vibration. If the FIRE energy were to disperse altogether, the body would have to vanish as it moved into non-existence and non-time.

By looking at the continuous shimmer of the FIRE elementals it is easy to see that all life is one: there is no break anywhere in the scintillating cloud surrounding everything. Each cloud of energy merges into those around it as far as the inner eye can see, and the whole of creation looks fluid and ethereal. The FIRE elementals are a very important part of the life process as they are literally omnipresent in their existence. As there can be no such thing as a cosmic vacuum, (that is, no place in the universe where life does not exist), there can be no place in the universe which does not have some of this elemental FIRE energy present in it. The main difference between all the various life forms in the universe is in the rate of the shimmering and the shade of the colouring.

Communication with FIRE elementals is best achieved by acknowledging and really believing that there is but one life in all things and using that universal brotherhood as a bridge. As has already been mentioned — but is worth emphasising again — 'all of life' includes everything from microbes to mountains, planets, stars and the interstellar dust of the universe itself. Thus, the FIRE elementals are really an extension of our own awareness and we can communicate with them much as we 'communicate' with our hands and feet, that is by simply willing them to act in a certain way. Of course, the 'certain way' chosen needs to be properly channelled, otherwise enormous amounts of willpower have to be put into the message transmission process, thereby causing a lot of distortion in the basic Lattice energy patterns. It is always possible to call up these very large amounts of power, but the price to be paid in terms of future karma is usually not worth the short-term benefits achieved.

The WATER elementals are less shimmery than those of FIRE, and form a sort of mist, bluish grey in colour. Paracelsis called them 'undines'. Whereas the programming of the FIRE elementals gives them the appearance of being forever inquisitive and outward moving, getting themselves into everything they can, the WATER elementals tend to keep themselves more to themselves and act in a less 'busy' manner. They can be imagined as a quiet pool with a misty surface, tranquil on top, but with a lot going on beneath. When we communicate with them in the right way, they are quick off the mark and very powerful. But, as WATER is the first of the polarisable energies, these elementals can either be helpful or obstructive. Sometimes they appear to take a fiendish delight in doing *exactly* what they are asked to do, irrespective of the consequences. Like modern computers, if you feed in an ambiguous or incorrect instruction, the resultant output can be both embarrassing and expensive. As WATER contains the basic ingredients of some human emotions, it is possible to communicate with these elementals using slightly more emotional picture language than is possible in the case of FIRE. They also interact positively with us at an intuitive level.

The elementals of AIR are as diaphanous as those of FIRE but without the shimmer; they are slightly yellowish in colour. We can communicate with them by means of more complex pictures than those for either FIRE or WATER because the element AIR contains the beginnings of mental ability. Paracelsis called them 'sylphs'. They are possibly the most difficult to control because, like the undines, they seem to delight in misinterpreting instructions and going off in all directions at once. This is of course only an interpretation of their actions based on our own human frustrations; they are no more capable of mischievous behaviour in reality than a computer is. Some form of elemental sheepdog, (if such a thing existed), would be ideal to keep them on the right path. As it is, a constant watch has to be kept on them, mainly because our minds are undisciplined and the AIR elementals can pick up that confusion. They are the elementals most concerned with bringing growth to fruition and are therefore more active in nature during the spring and summer. They are also especially active in schools, laboratories, libraries, and other places of learning and communication.

The elementals of EARTH are the ones with which we are most familiar, because they are the nearest devic life form to fairies and goblins. In fact, Paracelsis called them 'gnomes'. They do not have the physical forms of the much-loved entities of fairy stories, (unless you really want them to). Such figures exist purely in our imagination and only take on the physical form of our dreams if we put a lot of mental/emotional energy into their transformation. In normal life, EARTH elementals tend to group together in denser groups than the other three elemental forces, and can be imagined as greenish brown bundles of energy.

Communication is possible at a picture story language level, transmitting more complex ideas than is possible with the other elemental groups. Once started on a course of action, these EARTH energies are almost impossible to stop until they have finished what they were originally programmed to do; so make sure that your instructions are clear, correct and precise before transmitting them! Once again it must be emphasised that the elementals are not perverse or vindictive; they perform their tasks exactly as they are programmed and any errors are always found in the instructions.

The co-operation of the elementals is available to the whole of creation at all times. In fact, they are constantly performing their basic work of feeding the four fundamental cosmic energies to all parts of the Lattice. This is their cosmic programming which will continue whether humanity exists or not. (Even if all humanity were to be wiped out by some enormous world catastrophe, the flowers and trees would quickly take over again). In addition to their never-ending work with nature, the elementals can also be useful as part of the process geared to helping us understand and communicate with both the seen and unseen parts of the universe.

To some extent, we all have experience of these communicative abilities without being consciously aware of them.

Certain groups of people, such as healers, who work closer than most of us to the streams of the life-force, often use their 'feeling' of what is wrong with a patient to effect a cure, rather than relying on more logical clinical diagnosis. These feelings can be said to be messages from the elementals. The elementals are not consciously saying, 'This person has the beginnings of rheumatoid arthritis'; but the basic cosmic energy pattern differences disturb the normal elemental activities and these changes can be picked up by a sensitive healer. Looked at in a slightly different way, the elemental energies can be considered purely as the Lattice currents; and, as we are also a part of the continuous Lattice energies, we must have those same currents moving in us. The elementals can be said to form a sort of link between people and what we conventionally believe to be the individual physical bodies we inhabit.

This diagnostic energy pattern transfer technique is also available when dealing with inanimate objects. We all know people who are said to be 'good with cars' or 'a marvel at mending household gadgets'. These people are unconsciously communicating with the elemental forces which exist in those cars and gadgets. Once again, the proper energy patterns formed by the elementals are disturbed when the mechanism is not working correctly, and the cosmic energy fields emanating from it can be tuned into by sensitive people. The simple act of asking the car or television set what the problem is, (by trying to feel 'at one' with it), is often sufficient for the answer to appear in the questioner's mind. The elementals feeding life energies to all mechanisms are like small children: they benefit from love and affection, and they respond to kind words and gestures of appreciation. Even the simple act of giving a car or lawn mower a name can help to keep it working better. It strengthens our subconscious ties and hence our sympathetic Lattice resonances. (Once again it must be emphasised that the 'love and affection' offered to these inanimate objects is not an emotional bond, but simply an opening up to the reality of our common co-existence within the Lattice.)

The 'green fingers' of natural gardeners is another example of unconscious communication with the elemental kingdom. As was mentioned earlier, one of the most famous examples of this type of inter-relationship is the garden at the Findhorn Foundation in the north of Scotland. There, in the early 1960s a small group of nature-sensitive people grew remarkable vegetables and flowers on the inhospitable sand of a windswept and barren coastal caravan park. They communicated directly with the elementals and obeyed the instructions they were given without question. The result was that the sand yielded not just ordinary vegetables, but ones many times the size and quality of those grown in 'ideal' conditions in greenhouses and walled gardens nearby. Analysis by a Scottish university found the soil to be almost devoid of nourishment, so the analysers said a factor 'X' was involved — this factor being the extra care and devotion of the gardeners, who were properly 'tuned in' to their work with the elementals.

Angels and demons.

Whereas the elementals are the most basic form of devic life, at the other end of the scale are the archangels and archdemons. Angels and demons are the two aspects of the same sort of Lattice vibration used by Cosmos to communicate with the simpler forms of nature. In the passing of the years, since humans first recognised the existence of these beings, angels have become equated with good and demons with bad. As we are only human, we find it to be practically impossible to isolate ourselves from the ingrained teachings of society and religion, and therefore we consider *all* experiences either good and bad. In reality it will be easier for us to understand the true purpose of the whole cosmic structure if we were to learn how to replace these somewhat emotionally charged words with the less emphatic words 'help' and 'hindrance'. Even these alternatives are by no means ideal as they still contain patterns of desire, and an underlying religious bias. As has already been said, (and will no doubt be said again), the true simplicity and purpose of the path will only become apparent when all desires, including the desire for desirelessness, are abandoned. This is what Christ meant when he said that it was necessary to regain the state of being childlike in order to return to God.

For simplicity of explanation, the following description will be mainly about angels, but their demonic counterpart will be implicit in the discussion. Starting at the top level, the archangels are effectively the 'board of directors' of the devic kingdom, and are nothing like as approachable concerning mundane matters as are the elementals. Their job is to ensure that all the devic energies are properly distributed in the Lattice, and that the ordinary angels and underlings, (that is the fairies, elves, goblins, and others), perform their allotted tasks. This is an important and time-consuming job which leaves them little time to be concerned with other things. If the occasion is sufficiently important, they can be approached directly, just as the directors or vice-presidents of a public company can be approached directly if the situation is really crucial. (For those readers with computer skills, the archangels are similar to the main system software: they allocate the system resources).

According to which religious books we have studied, there are anything between three and twelve archangels and four and seven archdemons. Seven archangels seems to be the most popular number, with four particularly important ones. This is the right number so far as this book is concerned, because these four correspond with the four elements, (and also with the four cardinal points of the compass).

The archangel associated with FIRE and the south is St Michael. (Although given a masculine name and usually referred to as 'he', neither this archangel nor any other entity of the devic kingdom has a gender. Such designations are a carryover from religious tracts.) Michael has Yang* (outgoing) energy and is cosmically FIERY. For religious convenience this archangel is depicted in human form; but the real form is one of a shimmering energy field, intensely beautiful and slightly red in colour.

St Michael is considered to be the special protector of the Jews and is sometimes called 'god's vicegerent'. As FIRE is the first element to emerge from the cosmic Source, this relationship is to be expected. In Christian tradition, 'he' is considered the senior archangel; this is acknowledged by the full name of All Saints' Day — The Festival of St. Michael and All Angels. According to the Bible and the Koran, he is the leader of the angels when they march into battle, (as is described in the book of Revelations chapter 12, verse 7), and has up to 1,000 cherubim at his beck and call. (Cherubims are another form of devic energy. They perform special tasks for the senior angels.) St Michael is often depicted with a sword in his hand.

Many years ago there was a very serious and heated debate amongst the Christian bishops as to how many angels could stand together on the head of a pin. (Remember: angels are an accepted part of the Christian doctrine.) No conclusions were reached — which is just as well since an angel, being an energy field rather than a separate entity, is no more able of 'standing' on anything than a specific 'piece' of electromagnetism can. The physical size of the field is immaterial—it is the strength of it that counts.

The quality of the angelic energy field can be tuned into in exactly the same way as that of the simple elementals. It is possible at any time to call upon particular angels by con-

*A full explanation of the orientally based energies, Yin and Yang, is beyond the scope of this book. Basically, Yang energies are outgoing and active, while Yin energies are 'ingoing' and passive. FIRE and AIR are basically Yang, while WATER and EARTH are basically Yin.

centrating on the qualities desired, and trying to 'feel' those qualities becoming a part of our own being. What is happening at these times is that we are using our mind energy to vibrate the Lattice into the resonances which will sympathetically attract the devic energies, or qualities, which we require. Archangels require a far deeper level of concentration than elementals because their energy fields are less widespread and are also more highly tuned.

Of course, the same can be done with the demonic forces, which is why a strong diet of 'video nasties' is bad for the viewer's aura and subsequently for that person's outlook on life. By concentrating on the negative aspects of existence, video nasties viewers attract demonic energies and become bogged down in negativity themselves. The phrase 'mud sticks' is very true; for it is difficult to clean up an aura which has become very negative. The occasional brush with these negative forces does no harm; it is only prolonged exposure which sharpens the devic 'tuning' and attracts adverse energies.

It is worth remembering that a whole variety of ordinary angels are constantly available to be called to our aid at times of stress. There is always room for one or two more to sit on our shoulders, figuratively speaking. These angels will only remain for as long as they are required and should be positively released when they are no longer required. The release procedure is a simple 'thank you' to them and a visualisation of them leaving our surrounding energy field. The visualisation can either be of an entity similar to a human being, or of a body of coloured energy; use whichever feels more comfortable.

In terms of the Lattice, what we are doing when calling on these forces is using our WATER and AIR energies to resonate the Lattice into patterns which are sympathetic to the angelic qualities required. When those energies have served our purposes we disperse the patterns by consciously 'seeing' them break up.

Apart from the 'casual' angels which we can call on at any time, we each have special angels on a more permanent basis, known as 'guardian angels'. These special angels stay with us for long periods of time and help to regulate our resonances with the four elemental energies. They are our protectors in times of trouble. (Many people still say, 'His guardian angel is working overtime', when someone escapes an accident). This general protection does not mean that the angels continually protect their charge from bodily injury or even death, but rather that they try to ensure that the balance between the cosmic energies is kept at a level consistent with the karmic necessities of their charge's soul. Even when a person's aura is highly charged with demonic energies, the guardian angels are still there, trying to keep the Karmic energies flowing. To paraphrase the stickers seen in cars at Christmas, 'Guardian angels are for life, not just for Christmas': they arrive before birth and they remain until after death. The ones we have with us are those our soul energy chose as part of our preparation for life.

The majority of us are so unaware of what is going on in the real world of cosmic energies that we place ourselves in danger of destroying some of the progress we have made along our Path by insisting on moving against the energy stream. (In truth, this is our privilege and also our challenge because of our special gift of free-will). Our guardian angels try to filter the resulting adverse energy patterns into a strength with which we can cope. Even if the result of our ignorance is more than they can balance out and we die, the intervention of the angels will have helped us into a better state of balance in our next incarnation.

So Michael, the chief archangel, controls all these angelic processes; in terms of the Lattice, it means that this devic FIRE energy is a resonant part all the other devic energies and acts as the link between them and the highest cosmic energies, which are the primary source of life. The significance of his association with the south reflects the earthly equivalent of where the sun gives maximum energy at mid-day in the northern hemisphere; that is, where it is most FIERY. (The compass positions were associated with the archangels before the southern hemisphere was explored; therefore an anomaly exists concerning north and south. As the archangels do not actually stand in any particular geo-graphical position, the compass associations should be used simply as reminders of the respective angel's qualities.)

The second archangel is Gabriel. He controls the WATER element and the west, and vibrates with a bluish tint. His energy is Yin. Of the four main archangels, Gabriel is the one most directly associated with humanity. In Christian writ-ings, this is the angel who told Mary that she was to be the mother of Jesus. (Thus WATER energy polarised the Jewish community and gave it a major new faction.) In Islamic writ-ings, he is the angel who dictated the Koran to Mohammed. (Again, this is an energy of polarisation.) According to European folklore, Gabriel has a special trumpet upon which he will one day blow 'the last trump' and bring about the end of the world. (This job is bequeathed to another angel — St Israfil — in the Koran). Of course, Gabriel no more has a trumpet than Michael a flaming sword. They are both *energy fields*, not people, and all the paraphernalia with which they are associated simply illustrate the ways in which different cultures remember the basic abilities of the cosmic energies, usually without even knowing that such things exist.

The west is associated with Gabriel is because that is where the sun sets, before it is followed by the night and a time of rest. This is significant as Gabriel is an energy of peace. The west is also where the great ocean was as far as the early Europeans who categorised the angels were con-cerned. This explains the association of WATER with Gabriel

The third archangel is Raphael, the director of elemental AIR and guardian of the east. He is represented by the colour yellow and has Yang energy. The east is where the sun rises, creating a new day, and Raphael is associated with creativity. This is the angel who was befriended by Tobias, the son of Tobit and Anna, in the Apocrypha. Raphael can be translated as 'God heals' or 'God makes whole'. In the writings of Islam, Raphael was the angel who overcame the demon Asmodeus and banished him to the lower worlds.

The fourth archangel is Uriel, in charge of EARTH energy and positioned in the north. He is associated with the colour of greenish brown. There is no mention of Uriel in the Bible, or in the Apocrypha, but the Jewish books of Enoch are said to have been revealed to him by this archangel. (Enoch was the father of Methuselah and is mentioned several times in Genesis and also by St Luke, St Paul and St Jude). Uriel means 'Fire of God' and in folklore, he is associated with thunder and earthquakes, two energies which epitomise the EARTH nature of this devic being.

The other three archangels, according to Jewish writings, are Raguel, the 'avenger against planetary spheres'; Sariel, the 'avenger against sinning spirits'; and Remiel, the 'guardian of souls'. Islamic writings also include Israil, the angel of death, and Israfil, the angel of judgment. As far as the main cosmic energies are concerned, none of these archangels is as important as those associated with the four primary energies.

All the other devic entities are subservient to the four archangels, including Lucifer, who was the angel of light. According to legend, he challenged Michael for the position of God's vicegerent because he thought that he was the more important angel. He lost the fight and was banished to the lower world as a punishment for his pride. It is at this point in most of the Scriptures which describe angels and demons that the proper purpose of the elemental forces becomes confused with man-made judgments concerning good and evil. It needs to be reiterated that the devic kingdom is a kingdom of *energies* and that those energies do not have free-will: they operate exactly as they have been programmed to do, and any interpretation of the results of those actions as good or bad is simply a result of human misinterpretation. Clever religious leaders have been able to use this misinterpretation to control their congregations: they predict hellish tortures, meted out by the 'devils', to those who try to do anything which might upset their carefully calculated religious systems; and, of course, promise a life of bliss with the angels to the so-called 'good' people.

The whole subject of good versus evil is extremely complex, particularly as the operation of these forces in humans reacts primarily with the emotional body. To make the bold statement that there are really no such forces as good and evil not only makes the whole subject of morality too simplistic, but it also opens the way for righteous indignation from sincerely religious bodies. There *are* such forces as good and evil in the world, but they are man-made, not cosmically made. As far as Cosmos is concerned, there are simply four basic energies which vibrate in the strings of the Lattice and thereby regulate all manifestation. Then humankind came along and decided upon a 'purpose': all energies which appeared to aid that purpose were henceforth considered to be good, and all energies which seemed to hinder that purpose were seen to be bad. But Cosmos is unaffected by this arbitrary decision of 'purpose' and the subsequent categorisation of life into good and bad. Similarly are the devic forces unaffected. They continue to operate as programmed.

Thus, the entities we call demons are not cosmically evil; they simply pull us back towards the middle way from one type of excess, whilst the angels pull us back from another type of excess. We interpret these 'pull back' processes as good or evil dependent upon our agreement. This philosophy is not a license to do exactly what we want to do, because the overall regulator is karma. In the end, all that we do has to balance exactly, since the overall energy of the universe always balances and we are part of that universe.

The angels and demons are parts of that regulation process, which appears to move us either 'onwards' or 'backwards'. In fact, wherever we are and whatever we are doing is always exactly as it should be — neither good nor bad. It is not until after perfection has been achieved that a soul is able to view the experiences of pleasure and pain with equanimity. Talk of being wise after the event! However, knowing that these experiences are transitory offers a help in solving the apparently contradictory aspects of God's mercy versus pain and suffering.

The seven acknowledged archdemons have been coupled with the seven vices: so Lucifer rules pride; Mamon rules avarice; Asmodeus rules lechery; Satan rules anger; Beelzebub rules gluttony; Leviathan rules envy; and Belpheger rules sloth. Notice that three of the seven are names generally thought to be interchangeable, and signify the Devil — Satan, Lucifer and Beelzebub. They are, in fact, different aspects of the cosmic forces that jointly compose the complex energy we call the Devil. There can be no single all-powerful devilish entity on the same level as God, or Cosmos. (Cosmos has no opposite, being pure potential; whereas all devic energies are *active* and are associated with one or more of the four elements. Thus they are derived *from* Cosmos and cannot be equivalent.)

In between the angels and the elementals, there is a complex hierarchy of all the intermediate devic helpers. These have been described in folklore and legend even before writing was invented. Monotheistic religions tend to dismiss any thoughts of Nature Spirits because such ideas can clash with a simplistic teaching of the oneness of God. But there is actually no reason why the two philosophies cannot go hand in hand. The only proviso is that energies such as nymphs, goblins and salamanders should not be confused with the basic originating cosmic energy itself. It is reasonable to ask these entities for help, but we need not credit them with divinity.

Enough has now been said about this spectrum of cosmic energies to show that it is a useful and necessary part of the Lattice system. Without it, the world would not be able to function. It automatically operates the day-to-day Lattice energy interactions just as the heart and lungs of a human being continue to function without conscious effort. And just as those human functions can be modified by conscious thought if we so wish, so the devic functions can likewise be modified if the need arises.

The words 'fairy' and 'angel' can now be seen to be simply substitutes for what are, in reality, the primary energy patterns moving in the basic Lattice strings. Dependent upon temperament, some people prefer to deal with entities in human form such as angels, while others are more comfortable looking at the world from a more conventional and less controversial viewpoint. The main point to bear in mind is that these energies are available to help us in all that we do and can be contacted at any time. The communications can result in anything from the growing of healthier plants to the building of a better skyscraper. The elemental forces pervade the entire Lattice and are therefore available through all types of matter — animal, vegetable, and mineral.

Later on in this book, we will look at techniques available for easier communication with this important realm. But before reaching that point, we need to look at a few remaining aspects of the Lattice structure, particularly that associated with the way we interact with our environment.

Chapter 11

Emotional Energies

One of the most important features of the Lattice is that, from the viewpoint of time, it is a continuous storage system. All that has ever happened in the universe — all the physical, emotional, mental and spiritual events from the Big Bang to the present instant— have created vibrations in the Lattice strings; and, because there is no such thing as cosmic friction, those vibrations still exist. The amplitudes of the original Lattice nodal patterns have decreased with time as the energy wavefronts moved through the Lattice, but the patterns continue to exist, albeit at increasingly lower levels. The only way to cancel them is to vibrate the Lattice with the exact opposite pattern. This is one of the results of karma.

In some cases, when the originating energy is very strong or mainly composed of EARTH, the vibrations become 'locked' in closed patterns and remain at approximately their original strength. This is obvious with material structures such as buildings and mountains, but a similar locking feature can occur in both the emotional and mental planes. In the emotional plane, we sense these patterns as non-material presences such as ghosts and 'creepy feelings'; in one form in the mental plane, they represent the sum total of human knowledge, under a variety of banners such as 'Universal Wisdom' or the 'Akashic Records'.

The five normal human senses are our links with the material level of what we generally perceive as the 'Planetary Records', or the 'world around us' — what we see, hear, touch, smell, and taste. We get so used to communicating with our environment via these physical links that we often tend to forget that we have finer senses which have been specially developed over thousands of years for us to use as contacts with the higher planes. Lack of use makes these senses sluggish so that the ordinary person, brought up using just the ordinary senses, finds it difficult to spur the finer senses, such as the intuition, into action. The frustrating thing for our little-used finer tuned bodies is that the higher plane messages continue to impinge on our consciousness whether we sense them or not, just like sound waves continue to interact with a deaf person's ears. The brain continues to react to these signals even though our awareness or sensing mechanism is switched off.

Imagine the wealth of knowledge and information in which we are all immersed and which we presently fail to acknowledge! The history of the world is there; the details of each soul's incarnations; the emotional traumas of catastrophes; the heart-lifting moments of great achievements; the day-to-day memories of ordinary people, of saints and sinners. All that we do, say, think and feel causes vibrations in our own and other people's energy fields, and all that they say, feel and do affects our energy fields. We are all interconnected by the Lattice: there is no way around it. Thus, we can lead fuller and more purposeful lives if we become better acquainted with these Lattice mechanisms. The only requirements are for each of us to cultivate our finer senses and make fuller use of our normal five.

This is easier said than done, of course. There are some people who come into incarnation with a built-in ability to roam freely through the vast array of information and experiences locked in the Lattice around us. These people are 'seers', clairvoyants, psychics, etc. Their common bond is that they can tune in to the finer energies of the Lattice at will. The rest of us are occasionally startled by short periods of clarity when we suddenly find that an unexpected image or phrase appears in our mind out of the blue. These are occasions to be nurtured and investigated because it is on these occasions that the capacity for more continuous connection with the Lattice memory is built.

This book is not a manual on how to become a psychic; there are already plenty of books, courses and 'schools of the Wisdom' available for that. The purpose of this chapter is to make known, and to make more easily available, the great amount of information which is literally hanging in the space around us.

So first of all let's take a look at the phenomena of 'ghostly presences'. Many people don't 'believe' in ghosts despite the thousands upon thousands of recorded instances of their appearances. The Society for Psychical Research has a library full of sightings, yet many people, especially conventional scientists, will go to great lengths to produce convoluted explanations for what are by no means rare occurrences. Often these explanations are more far-fetched than a simple belief in the ghosts would be. It is certainly true that many of the records are either stories made up by people seeking glory, or other illusions of one sort or another. But this cannot apply to *all* the records gathered by dedicated and experienced field officers. There are too many which are not explained in any reasonable way. Because these accounts are not explainable as the result of electromagnetic effects, scientists often say that the observers were misled or suffered from hallucination. Furthermore, these events seldom appear on photographs because photographic emulsions can only react to specific parts of the electromagnetic spectrum. Apparitions are generated within the *emotional* spectrum of the Lattice and are transparent so far as electromagnetic sensing apparatus is concerned. Very occasionally, the emotional energy is so strong that it sympathetically resonates a small part of the electromagnetic spectrum and will appear as a vague image on photographs.

However, non-electromagnetic energies are visible normally to those people who are sensitive to this particular part of the Lattice overall spectrum: people such as clairvoyants and other psychics. As said earlier, science has not yet devised a machine to replace human beings or animals as the sensors for these emotional vibrations. Because they *are* based on emotional energy it is often the case that the people who can see them are also highly emotional. This makes communication between down-to-earth scientists and clair-voyants a difficult process and misunderstandings are com-mon. Nevertheless it is frustrating that this wide spectrum is available for investigation, and yet there are so few open-minded people available to take up the challenge. If rumours are to be believed, (and they often contain grains of truth), various governments have experimented in these areas in the past, and may still be doing so — for example, *The Philadelphia Experiment* — but their interest lies only in discovering ways of keeping one step ahead of their ene-mies. Such experiments only consider a narrow part of the whole field, and are generally abandoned early on because funding is removed when quick results are not achieved. Yet a fairly low budget and long-term investigations into Lattice energies would pay dividends in the end, and might even lead to the discovery of an alternative measuring device to replace the present and essential human interface.

The common characteristic of ghostly presences in the Lattice is that they were originally generated by very large discharges of emotional energy. This is why they usually occur in places where there have been sudden or traumatic death or deaths. The ghosts haunting old castles or moaning down the corridors of ancient mansions are generally the emotional remains of people who were executed, murdered or otherwise done to death in particularly shocking ways. The sad thing about these apparitions is that they desperate-ly want to dissolve so that the EARTH-locked soul can con-tinue on its path to perfection. But so long as some of the energy from a previous incarnation is held captive in a ghostly energy pattern, the soul is not able to continue its journey. The emotional energy generated by the frightened people who see these pitiful beings helps to boost the circu-lating EARTH energy locked in their ghostly patterns and this makes matters even worse. Thus these poor souls sometimes remain unreleased for hundreds of years.

It used to be a common duty of the church to perform ceremonies of release — exorcism — for ghosts and other so-called malign influences. But once again modern religious teachings have clouded the issue; and most present-day priests do not believe that these unfortunate semi-beings actually exist. This means that the phantoms either have to continue haunting the earth until a more enlightened age returns, or that they will eventually fade down to a level where the soul is able to compromise part of its next incarnation in order to nullify the vestiges of its previous emotional experience. In the cases of strong energy fields, this process may take a thousand years or more. So — if you meet a ghost, try to offer it compassion rather than fear. This will help to reduce the locking field. *Apparitions can do no harm to those who do not connect with them emotionally.*

In fact apparitions cannot harm *anyone* directly. Any troubles which result from such an encounter are caused by a common emotional bonding taking place. The more the compassion and less the fear present at the time of meeting, the less the amount of emotional transfer. Thus, by keeping a detached but loving energy flowing within the viewer's own aura, no 'old' energy can leak from the apparition to the viewer and no new emotional energy can be fed to enhance the field that has been locked. It sounds difficult, but now that you know what a ghost really is, the process might be easier to achieve.

Another form of emotional energy in the Lattice is that commonly known as the poltergeist. This manifestation is usually coupled with the idea of ghosts, though in reality they have an entirely different cause. Whereas ghosts are the patterns resulting from strong emotional experiences of (usually) dead people, poltergeists are always caused by living beings — generally young females reaching puberty. A characteristic of these particular girls is that they have extremely strong emotional energies (which don't necessarily show on the surface), and the patterns that they unconsciously generate spill over into uncontrolled physical activity which manifests itself as psycho-kinesis. (Psychokinesis is the movement of inanimate objects without the use of physical connections.) At a conscious level, the perpetrators have no knowledge of the effects of their emotions and are as bewildered and frightened as the ordinary people around them when small objects go flying through the air, mirrors crack, and doors slam unaided. The energy is usually destructive and noisy, and the manifestations stop when the girl reaches puberty.

There are other forms of psychokinesis which are less destructive than poltergeists and experiments have been going on for many years in various scientific laboratories in order to harness these aspects of the Lattice. Some of these are discussed in the next chapter.

Any level of the Lattice energy can be affected by waveforms generated at a lower level. For example, thought energy can, and often does, produce emotional patterns, and emotional energy can alter physical things. In fact, energy waves at any level *automatically* generate sympathetic waves at all lower levels. Spiritual waves affect the three lower levels — mental, emotional and physical — thought waves affect the emotional and physical levels; and emotional waves affect the physical level. The process does not work in reverse. For example, physical waves do not sympathetically produce emotional waves, and emotions cannot directly affect the way people think. (People in emotional turmoil sometimes say 'I'm so upset I can't think straight.' This is not a case of emotion directly affecting thought; what is happening is that the whole body's energy system is out of balance and the thought processes are confused as a result of that unbalance.

Thus cosmic energies are normally transmitted downwards from the spiritual to the physical. Our function as human beings is to take those energies and to transform them back into the spiritual level, and beyond to Cosmos itself. We do this by becoming more spiritually aware. We can take some of our day-to-day energies which reside in the lower manas and use the bridge between the lower and higher minds to transfer energy into the higher manas. (Refer to Figure 4 in chapter 6.) Thus we each use the experiences of our personality to enrich our soul.

Let's look at the downward transformation process in more detail. If you look at the process by which you produce anything — a meal, a walk in the woods, a new motorcar — you will find that it follows a standard system of steps. First of all there must be the desire to do whatever it is. Then there must be the idea of how to do it. Then enthusiasm, however small, is required to motivate the body, and then the actual action. The process always happens like that. The initial desire level occurs as an interaction between spirit and thought. It is not an emotional desire at this stage because spirit is emotionless: it is more a vague wanting or knowing that such and such needs to be done. Then this desire moves into the mental realm and strengthens into a clearer idea of what is required. Thought waves are generated from the previous 'desire' waves and a nodular pattern is formed at this mental level with the possible form of the finished product. (Even a walk in the woods is a 'product'.) At this stage, the emotions come into play, and the more recognisable 'wanting' occurs. 'I want to do this' or 'I do not want to do that'. If the pattern is positive, the emotional waves vibrate the physical level to action and an actual result is achieved. If the pattern is negative, no physical pattern is generated and the energy of the previous levels is abandoned.

Consider this from the point of view of the four basic energies: firstly the process must have life, (FIRE), that is, it must exist; then there must be a desire to do the thing, (WATER); then the creative process comes into being, (AIR).

Finally the result is achieved, (EARTH).

If the process is aborted, it does not necessarily vanish immediately. Dependent on the power of the desire and thought that was generated, it may continue as a Lattice pattern for some time. However, if a person continually abandons half-finished projects, the patterns from these can form a confusing and clogging cloud in the aura around that person, thereby making it more and more difficult to formulate and complete any project in the future. We all know people who are full of great ideas but take no action. And we also know people of whom we say, 'They talk a lot but never seem to say anything.' These are examples of unfinished Lattice processes. The more someone generates these partial patterns, the more difficult it becomes to follow a complete path from spirit to matter. The hazy energy patterns use up part of the person's total energy quota and get in the way of further formulations. What is needed in these cases is either a cleaning-out course, or properly directed energy streams — such as some form of meditation, coupled with physical exercises directed along special cleansing paths at all levels; or the assistance of someone who can see when the energy stream moves into well-worn paths, and can help to direct it into new channels. Unfortunately, the people with the 'stuck' energies have generally got to the point of such confusion that they do not recognise their need.

The same debilitating energy patterns occurs with '-holics' (alcoholics, workaholics, etc.). In these cases, the emotional Lattice patterns have become very fixed and most of the energies coming down are diverted into the strong vortices of 'habit'. Habits in general are Lattice patterns which have become so fixed that they automatically absorb most of the energies near them: just like whirlpools, they suck nearby currents into their self-centred sphere of activity and add them to their already too strong patterning. Breaking these vortices is a difficult business, as anyone with a strong habit will confirm. But, following the rule that all changes have to follow from spirit to matter, the *desire* to break the habit has to be there, otherwise no permanent change can occur. For instance, this can be seen when someone, as a result of nagging, or peer pressure, agrees to give up smoking. The habit may appear to be controlled but eventually the person will start smoking again. (Parts of the pattern remain and ultimately overcome the pressures imposed by other people.) Only when the strong desire of the person who wants to stop smoking is at the head of the chain of events will the vortex be able to disperse entirely. Organisations such as Alcoholics Anonymous recognise the importance of a desire to reform and require it as a prerequisite for membership.

Having read this far, it should be clear that the Lattice patterns are the main system by which we operate on a day to day basis. If we understand the Lattice procedures, many of the difficulties and riddles of everyday life will disappear. The train of events always starts with desire and moves through thought to emotional need and thence to action. No stage can be left out and if the train is broken the final stabilising stage will not occur. The patterns formed by the Lattice nodes at each step may sometimes be very strongly bonded and leave a distorted after-image which can exist for a long time. These after-images always slow down future patterning and make increased awareness more difficult to achieve. The main purpose of the Buddhic search for desirelessness is to cancel all the after-images that clutter each soul's aura. The desirelessness they seek is mainly based on desire at an *emotional* level: spiritual desires are far easier to disperse because they do not contain the inertia of EARTH energy. Once all forms of desire have gone, thoughts and actions become transitory and a clear path to spirit can be firmly established.

This chapter has concentrated mainly on emotional patterns that can be difficult to disperse. In the next chapter, we will look at the thought patterns which surround us at all times and see how they also affect our lives. These two classes of energy — thoughts and emotions — are the ones we live with every day, and they are the ones we most need to understand. Because they are confused in most of us they are instrumental in making us see ourselves merely as goats. Eventually our clearer vision will let us to see our tigerness.

Chapter 12

Thoughts and Memories

By now it should be fairly clear that most human beings operate at two distinct levels. The everyday functions are run by the personality, that part of a human being which consists of the lower mind, emotions and the physical body — the lower manas. These are made up mainly of AIR and EARTH energies and are sometimes called the astral, etheric and physical bodies. The energy which drives these comes from the soul or ego level, and consists of the higher mind, the atma and the buddhi — the higher manas. The atma is universal spirit, (FIRE); the buddhi is universal love and intuition, (WATER); and the higher mind is aspiration and aesthetic stimulation, (AIR). Although these upper three energies are the ones which really control our lives, we are generally only conscious of the lower three. This is because the peak of the personality triangle, (see figure 4 in chapter 6), is the lower mind or manas and it is ruled by logic and time. Going back to the story of the tiger in chapter 1, the personality is similar to the goat which we think we are, and the soul includes the energy of the tiger which is trying to make its presence known. The more we become aware of our total Lattice pattern, the easier it becomes to strengthen the bridge between the higher and lower manas, thereby making it easier to recognise our tigerness as we move confidently along the path back to the Source.

The mental energy of the lower manas in the Lattice is very strong and is connected to patterns of the memories of all the wisdom of the universe. Everything that has ever been done or is going to be done is stored in the Lattice mental energies. The saying that 'there is nothing new under the sun' is very true at this level: practically all the inventions and innovations produced by humanity already exist as patterns in these universal memory banks. Most of them have been made and tried before, either by previous civilisations on Earth, or in other parts of the galaxy. (We'll be talking about other world inhabitants and intergalactic communication in the next chapter.)

The present-day vogue for 'channelling' is actually the channellers tapping into this enormous store of information. This does not belittle the results achieved by these people: the very fact that they are able to connect clearly with this source is a tremendous bonus for humanity at large. And the fact that they see their connections not as their own direct efforts but rather as the efforts of advanced beings feeding the information to them simply increases their confidence and makes the interchanges stronger. The mechanism is rather like the baby elephant Dumbo's feather. He didn't believe he could fly without his feather; nor do channellers believe in their innate abilities. They feel that they are unable to operate without the support of their 'source'. The point to note is that we are *all* able to connect directly with similar sources and, in fact, we do so far more than we consciously realise. Precognition, synchronicity, déjà-vu and intuition are all forms of these interchanges at work.

The question sometimes raised is, 'How can we know that these sources are good rather than evil? Murderers and serial killers sometimes claim that they are directed by internal voices too.' This is quite true: there are all sorts of messages coming from the Lattice because it contains *all* experiences. So the 'bad' ones are there as well as the 'good' ones. But, remembering what we said in the previous chapter about our sympathetic resonances, the average person's 'receiving' system will not vibrate very strongly to thoughts of murder or sadomasochism. It is only when these energies already exist at a personality level that they will be 'picked up' and recognised by a potential criminal. A strong diet of video nasties and reading material describing horrific killings makes the reader's personal resonances ripe for exploitation by similar energy patterns which already exist in the Lattice thought-waves. This is why, if we spend some time each day dwelling on our capacities for healing the world and loving our fellow beings, we will strengthen these vibrations within our personality and attract others to us.

Accessing the different energy patterns within the mental level of the Lattice requires different amounts of training and clarity of thought. The intuitive section is always open to all of us — the only requirement for its recognition is for the recipient not to be too tied into logical thought patterns. Looked at from the viewpoint of primary energies, intuition is a WATER energy and thought an AIR one. So the intuitive messages come to us at a higher level than thoughts; but they cannot be recognised until we 'translate' them into thoughts and this mental energy is closely allied to logic. As most intuitive messages appear at first reading to be illogical, our minds immediately censor and do not acknowledge the intuitive communications at all. Thus, though we are continually bombarded by clear intuitive messages, very few of them actually filter through to our everyday consciousness.

Intuition is not specifically a 'female' energy. The phrase 'feminine intuition' is well known, and it is often thought that women are much more intuitive than men. As has been shown above, we are *all* given intuitive messages all the time; we all have buddhic energy in our upper triangle. However, the way in which the energies are distributed in the lower triangle means that women tend to be less logical then men. Women in general regard the world around them as more of a 'magical' place than men do. They are more accepting of what 'is' and less concerned with the how and why of 'is-ness'. Therefore female mental processes are less censorious and intuition gets a chance to be heard. This statement is not meant to contain any sexist bias — it is as much a fact as saying that men generally have more body hair than women, or that women have higher voices.

If men could learn to rely less on logic, they could be equally intuitive. In fact, the type of person who uses intuition as a daily tool is often an inventor or innovator, who is frequently classed as an eccentric. The art of invention is to ignore logic, and to come up with what appear to be ridiculous solutions at first sight. Most inventors spend a great deal of their time being ridiculed by less forward-thinking colleagues. No doubt it was considered a good Sunday afternoon's entertainment to go out to Kittihawk and watch the Wright brothers trying to get their large and heavy apparatus into the air. 'How can they expect something like that to fly . . . . it doesn't even flap its wings.' And I have no doubt that cavemen doubled up with mirth as they watched the poor misguided fool trying to fit slices of tree trunks onto his sledge when everyone knew that the best way of moving loads was, and always had been, by dragging them.

But these inventors had intuitive communications from the universal wisdom within the Lattice, (whether they realised it or not), and the mental patterns for aeroplanes and wheels had become firmly implanted in their personal memory banks. The sympathetic resonances of parts of their individual mental energies had been triggered by corresponding patterns already existing in the larger Lattice patterns, and images of unknown mechanisms were the result. Because we seldom sense these communications clearly, the visions we get have essential bits missing or are, at best, out of focus. So the frustrated inventors burn the midnight oil to fill in the blanks or vagaries in their futuristic designs, while their friends smile benignly and hope that they will soon regain their senses. It has always been like this from way before the pyramids were built, (look at the design modifications made during the construction of those mighty works), and way before the foundations of Atlantis were laid. And it will continue to be like this until we learn to accept that intuition is a useful part of our total make-up and not something which is more of a laugh than a real help.

The obvious question now arises: 'If women are more intuitive, why are most inventors men?' The simple answer is that the intuitive messages, once received, have to then be translated into a logical format before they can become practical. Remember the elemental sequence for all products; life, (FIRE), goes to desire, (WATER), thence to creativity, (AIR), and finally to construction, (EARTH). With women, the WATER level is strong, manifesting itself in the intuitive messages, but translation into logical systems is not. With men, creativity is so strong that it usually blocks out WATER energy; but if, as in the case of inventors, it does filter down, practical AIR/EARTH energies will follow through.

The reticence of humanity in general and men in particular to accept intuition as a useful tool is part of the syndrome concerning our inability to *prove* so-called unscientific events (see chapter 1). 'Feelings' are all very well but they are not considered good substitutes for hard facts. It is interesting to note that dowsers and seers are sometimes used by hard-headed business organisations and police forces when deduction and logic have produced no answers. The results that these psychic people produce are seldom 100 per cent accurate, so their assistance is really only called upon as a last resort. If they are successful in finding hidden waterways, seams of metallic ores, or kidnap victims, then they are 'lucky', but if they fail, then their efforts occasion smirks from the doubters and murmurs of 'I told you so'. Neither psychics nor doubters are to be blamed: interchange with the mental plane is still a hit and miss affair and our job is to improve intuitive techniques until they are acceptably reliable. Knowledge of the Lattice and the way it works can do a lot to help this process.

So let's look at the mechanism of the Lattice at the mental level and see how the interchanges might be cultivated more effectively.

Expanding slightly on the general way that energy moves

through the Lattice, we see that desire, (the vision or dream), goes through thought, (the creative idea), via emotion, (the will to act), to the physical object, (the final result). The latter two are a splitting of EARTH energy into its more usual human divisions. The clearer the thought level is, the better the final product will be. But if the creative idea stage is muddled, then the final product will not function correctly either. When the original desire is manifested, it produces sympathetic resonances in the mental plane, which automatically highlight all the past experiences of that particular desire. Thus, the memory banks in the Lattice of the 'universal mind' underline all events of a similar nature in the same way that a specific smell or colour causes the human brain to bring forward all memories evoked by that particular experience.

We will all remember times when an event *nearly* brought forth the memory of something else, but it was not possible to bring that vague memory fully into focus. And we know that trying to force the memory to become clearer only caused frustration — it still stayed just out of reach. The best course is to leave the half-formed memory at the edge of one's awareness and get the brain to concentrate on something else; then, all of a sudden, the focus on the vague memory sharpens and the whole experience comes flooding back. The same applies to the system of obtaining information from the 'universal store'. It takes time for the human brain to come into proper resonance with the messages being given to it and the best way to aid the process is to relax into it. It is too tight a focus that slows the process down. This is much the same as the example given in chapter 5 concerning the best way to see elemental energy: we should use our peripheral vision. Similarly the ability to recognise the half-formed ideas resides in the parts of the brain which look at the overall scene rather than at the fine details. Listening to some music, reading a novel, going for a walk, etc. are ways in which to widen that focus, and allow nature to take its own course. Some of the greatest inventions have come when inventors were admiring the sunset, watching cricket on the village green, or sitting dozing under an apple tree after a good lunch of venison!

The golden rule to remember at all times is that living Life, interchanging energies with the Lattice, and becoming more aware of one's inherent godliness is all part of smelling the roses along the path. None of them are to be taken too seriously. Excessive seriousness simply stiffens one's individual Lattice patterns at all levels and it then becomes increasingly difficult to keep the interchanges flowing freely. This is one of the main reasons for the human aging process: as all life energy originates at the spiritual level and has to filter down to the physical one via the other levels, stiffness of thought or emotions — habits, prejudices, bigotry, etc. — cause a corresponding stiffening of the physical body which we see as such illnesses as arthritis, rheumatism, sciatica, hardening of the arteries, etc.

On the other hand, it is ill-advised to be so lackadaisical that nothing is ever achieved. Excessive sloppiness at any level stops the energies from ever becoming properly focussed. Thus we see many so-called 'laid-back' people who are total non-achievers. They may live longer than the stiff people, but what they do in their lives does not move them further along their path back to the Source. It is worth remembering that this is the whole purpose of existence: to return to the Source; or, to put it another way, to become so aware of Cosmos in the Lattice gaps that we can cross back over the Zero energy barrier and return to our origins. All the explanations and comments in this book are geared to helping each one of us with this process.

Having reiterated the important purpose of this book, let us now look at some of the other facets of the Lattice energy in the mental plane.

We will examine telepathy first. Telepathy can be defined as the ability of a sentient being to transmit and/or receive non-electromagnetic messages without using any of the normal five senses. ('Sentient beings' include animals, as some of these are highly telepathic.) There are thousands of instances of this form of communication at work, but there is no universally accepted scientific explanation. Many laboratory experiments have been undertaken, especially during the middle of this century, to try to prove conclusively that Extra Sensory Perception (ESP) actually exists. The results are interpreted by some as conclusive proof of the existence of ESP and by others as either 'not proven' or else as badly conducted experiments. The plain fact is that people who rely on the electromagnetic spectrum, conventional relativity, or quantum theory to give the answer to all manifestations in the universe cannot bring themselves to accept that there may possibly be other energies of which they are unaware. So it is a waste of time trying to persuade them to change their minds.

On the other hand, acceptance of new ideas must be tempered with a healthy scepticism if gullibility is to be avoided. There is a narrow path to be trodden between the two extremes. This is why you, the reader, are asked not to accept all that is written here as the absolute Truth, nor to dismiss it as pure fantasy either, but to test it against your other knowledge and experiences. Is it reasonable? Are there other instances that come to mind of similar things? How do these new ideas feel? Are there any of your own experiences that contradict what is written here? It is the responsibility of each one of us to make these tests and then to accept or reject anything new put before us. That is a necessary part of being a self-actuated and responsible human being.

Telepathy causes conventional scientists a lot of problems. It doesn't obey the normal laws of electromagnetic radiation in that the power of the transmission does not always decrease with distance. And it doesn't seem to obey the rule of relativity which says that nothing can travel faster than light. Both of these are valid objections for any transmission that propagates at a purely physical level. But telepathy propagates through the Lattice in the *mental* plane. At this level, the law about the speed of light does not apply. All thought transmissions are non-physical and can therefore travel many times faster than light waves. Nor does their intensity automatically decrease with distance. They are more like laser light in that they can be focussed on a particular recipient with practically no reduction of the originating energy level. Also, because they do not contain any physical energy, the amount of power required for their transmission is very low. Thus, a good telepathic transmitter can effortlessly and simultaneously send messages to recipients in several widely spaced areas.

The actual transmission is, of course, vibrations of the Lattice strings at the mental level. These can be received by anyone sufficiently attuned to them. Such transmissions emanate all the time from every human being. The Lattice is awash with thoughts racing hither and thither in the same way that the space around us, (and within us), is awash with radio, television and radar transmissions all the time. We are not generally aware of them because our bodies are insensitive to signals at radio frequencies. (There are occasional reports of people hearing radio transmissions through the fillings in their teeth, but this is only because the metallic fillings have minute faults in them which turn them into radio receivers.)

Even with the help of a radio receiver, we don't hear all the transmissions simultaneously because the receiver is 'tuned' to a particular frequency in order to receive only the signal transmitted at that frequency. For example, if a radio is tuned to 200 kilohertz (kHz) it will receive only the BBC 200 kHz long wave transmission. It will not process transmissions from other radio transmitters unless they are also broadcasting at 200 kHz. But all the other thousands of signals are still there, around and inside that radio receiver. A badly designed radio will receive several different transmissions at the same time, which we hear as 'interference' or garbled speech in the background while we are trying to listen to the station we want. Similarly, the human brain is capable of 'tuning into' thought transmissions. Generally, untrained minds pick up a hotchpotch of signals at the same time — just like the cheap radio receiver, their tuning is too broad. However, it is possible to train the mind to tune more precisely to particular transmissions. The trick is to focus the mind on a unique characteristic of the transmitting person. This creates sympathetic patterns in the 'receiving' energy fields, which will exactly match those of the person sending the signals. This is exactly what a radio receiver does: the receiving 'tuned circuits' are duplicates of the transmitting ones.

Telepathy is now being seriously investigated by many government-sponsored research establishments throughout the world. The volume of information available concerning possible times when telepathy has been the only logical explanation for a communication 'out of the blue' is too large to ignore. Some experiments are from human to human and some involve animals such as dolphins. The original experiments conducted by Professor Rhein at Princeton University between the 1940s and 1970s were mainly to decide whether telepathy is fact or fiction. The experiments being conducted now are to see if this phenomenon can be safely and reliably harnessed.

Rhein's original experiments, and those being conducted now, also embrace an offshoot of telepathy — precognition. This is considered by many scientists to be 'off the wall' because it smacks of magic and fortune telling. Basically, precognition is knowing about something before it occurs, so it is easy to understand why scientists are uncomfortable with it. At first glance,it opens up a Pandora's box full of fantasies such as time-travel, witchcraft and similar unscientific possibilities.

In fact, time is not folded back on itself or distorted in any way. It is our *view of time* that is distorted. As long as we go on considering time to be a linear and continuous phenomenon, unexplainable experiences will continue to embarrass us. But we know from the early chapters of this book that time is neither continuous nor does it necessarily propagate at an equal rate throughout the universe. (The 'edge' of the universe may be where the rate of propagation has slowed down to nil.) Furthermore, we now know that the space around us contains a store of information concerning what we have done, *and what we are likely to do.* (Remember the simile of the billiard balls.) The Lattice contains all the energies of our existence in the form of vibrations and nodal patterns. And these multiple happenings are interacting all the time with those of others around us. Considered at the level of the Lattice, the whole of space is filled with crossing ripples much like those in a pond into which gangs of boys have thrown handfuls of pebbles.

The time at which we sample the happenings around us is not necessarily either continuous or linear. The logical brain tries hard to make it so because this makes the personality feel secure. (The majority of what we do is directed towards making the personality feel secure.) But we have the option of sensing parts of the Lattice that are not in a convenient time sequence as far as personality is concerned. Some people have a greater ability than others — in common parlance, they 'see the future'. What they see is not necessarily an unchangeable future because we have the choice to modify the forthcoming Lattice patterns, (that is, the patterns which are liable to interact with our personal ones). Generally we don't bother to do this. Firstly, because we are not sufficiently aware to see them coming, and secondly, because the consequences of one small change can be too large to contemplate even if we did. (Remember the dictator and his breakfast jam.) No, we let the future take its natural course except in cases of dire emergency when we summon up the energy to modify the Lattice patterning and hope that the re-arrangement will be to our advantage. (This can be in the short term, but because karma needs to keep things balanced, it will eventually revert to its original path — perhaps in a future lifetime.)

The precognitive people who took part in Rhein's experiments had the ability to predict the sequence of ESP cards which had not yet been chosen. The five basic ESP cards had individual drawings of a cross, a circle, a square, three wavy lines and a star on them. The basic test was for the 'transmitter' to look at the cards in sequence and for the blindfolded 'receiver' to write down what they felt the viewer was looking at. In some tests, it was found that the receiver was writing down sequences of cards not yet chosen. Several people tested had this ability, but were not always able to control the time gap.

So, with our new knowledge we can see that precognition may be our own distortion of what is in the mental level of the Lattice patterning. Proper control of this form of Lattice viewing is much more difficult than simple telepathy, and requires an ability not only to focus clearly on particular Lattice patterns but also to 'sweep' through those patterns and select specific time sequences. Such an ability is not generally useful to the average person. Telepathy is a far more helpful tool to cultivate.

The final phenomenon associated with the mental level that we will deal with is psychokinesis. This is the ability to move or produce material objects by the use of the mind and without the use of any intermediate physical tools. Instances of this phenomenon range in action from the miracles of Christ to the manifestation of *verbhuti* (pronounced 'verbooti'), a perfumed grey powder, by Sai Baba, and the movement of objects encased in a bell jar by a Russian lady named Kalagina in 1967. (This last instance is recorded on an old grainy black and white film held in the BBC archives.)

We have records of the miracles of Christ in the four

gospels and other writings of the early Christian era. We have numerous eyewitness accounts of Sai Baba producing verbhuti by rubbing his fingers and thumb together and also of him producing solid objects from between his out-stretched hands. Sceptics can call it sleight of hand, (and frequently do so). I have personally seen Sai Baba produce the grey powder several times while I was visiting his ashram in India. I have also seen other examples of his power, such as the production of a sweet nectar from a stone which resides in a children' home he sponsored many miles from the ashram. Visitors are allowed to hold this stone and produce the nectar themselves. Sai Baba does not need to be present. I have seen nectar appear from the stone in my hand and, after the stone was returned to its box, the palm of my hand continued to generate nectar, (which I periodically licked off), for a further twenty minutes. Another member of the party I was with was still producing nectar after three-quarters of an hour. Let me hasten to add that I am *not* a devotee of Sai Baba and left his ashram after a couple of days because I found it so uninspiring, but I do believe that the manifestations I saw were genuine and that the man is all he purports to be — though not necessarily what his followers would have him be!

Those who do not believe that such happenings are possible will never be convinced and there is no point in wasting energy trying. But for the more open-minded, psychokinesis can be considered from the point of view of the interplay of the Lattice energies. It is part of the normal mechanism that starts with desire and finishes with a material effect. The difference in this case is that the material effect is not dependent on other material effects before it. The more normal sequence would be for the mind to direct tools to form the scented powder out of specific ingredients. In the case of psychokinesis, the mind uses the energy within the Lattice and re-form it directly as matter — a sort of atomic fusion process but without the radiation hazards or spectacular fireworks.

Obviously this is not something that anyone can do. Masters such as Christ and Sai Baba really understand the processes involved and know that a really clear and direct chain of command is necessary for the system to work properly. A proper understanding of the purpose and function of time is also required. Remember also that there is an emotional subsection to the physical level. Unless this is absolutely spotless, some of the clutter of unresolved emotions will interfere with the transformation process and, instead of verbhuti being produced, the operator will probably become extremely ill. As the majority of people would only try to use psychokinesis for self-glorification, there would inevitably be some muddied emotions present and the experiment would be doomed to failure.

The same goes for moving objects at a distance. One of the reasons why laboratory experiments concerning this phenomenon usually fail is because the performer is being asked to prove his/her worth. So there is some pride or indignation somewhere in the process and this is sufficient to block the pathway.

Sceptics will be saying 'Excuses, excuses!'; and I have no response to such comments. It is up to you, the reader, to apply the tests mentioned previously and to decide if the explanations given here are reasonable. This process of analysis should be going on throughout the book.

Having touched on the subjects of miracles and magic, it will be worthwhile looking at these phenomena in more detail. The next chapter will be devoted to this task.

Chapter 13

Masters, Miracles and Magic

Human beings have always been fascinated with events which seem to be beyond rational explanation. We have a love/hate relationship with them because we envy the power they exhibit, but are frightened by that power as well. We are mainly governed by logic and a need for security, therefore everything has to have a reason. Unreasonable things are threatening and scary and need to be accounted for to give us peace of mind. So that bump, bump, bump in the night has to be investigated, dragging us from a warm bed to make sure that there isn't a back door swinging in the breeze following the entry of a lazy burglar. Similarly, people who can manifest things out of thin air, foretell the future, perform instant cures or turn lead into gold are a subconscious threat and must be categorised and put into safe boxes labelled 'stage magician', 'hypnotist', or 'charlatan'. If they don't fit the definitions, they leave us feeling uncomfortable, and we say that the facts we were given must have been incomplete, then we stuff the offending party away in a box marked 'faulty facts'. After that we can breathe easily again: all the worrying questions have been solved and the world is once more a safe place.

But . . . . this isn't reality. It is simply a scheme to give us a sense of false security. In reality there *are* people who can manifest things out of thin air, who can foretell the future and who can perform instant cures. They should be put in a special box marked 'Masters' or 'Avatars'. The term 'Master' includes both male and female. Just as souls are sexless and reincarnate as either male or female depending on the needs of karma, so Masters, being advanced souls, comprise the attributes of both sexes. Avatars are advanced souls who no longer operate through the lower bodies of the personality.

They generally concentrate on enhancing a particular aspect of the higher Lattice energies, but sometimes return to the world as humans, such as Christ or Mother Meera. Masters achieve perfection during their lifetime; avatars are already perfect when they return to help us.

Of course, for every genuine Master there are thousands of masqueraders. The charlatanism and misdeeds of the thousands cloud our judgment concerning the few genuine articles. This is a pity because these special people have a lot to pass on to us if we ask them sincerely. They are not free to push their special gifts onto people who do not express a willingness to receive them. If you ever find a 'Master' who tries to convert you into believing in his/her doctrines or special powers, beware! Such people are not the genuine article. Demonstration is fine, but persuasion is not part of the scheme of things. It upsets the Lattice balance. True Masters say, 'Here is what I have to offer. It is up to you whether you take it or leave it.' Then they move on, allowing the observers total freedom of choice.

One of the main functions of a Master is to keep the purer Lattice energies vibrating by acting as a special resonator. Thus, many Masters have a 'Buddha-field' surrounding them which can be easily sensed by people who are psychic and by the majority of sentient animals. It can also be sensed by people who are not psychic, but they generally feel it as just a sense of peace and well-being. This field is a source of spiritual energy and those who move into it benefit even though they often don't realise that changes are happening. Thus, some Masters have 'ashrams' which usually offer an open invitation to people to stay for a week or two and to take part in various spiritual practices. Very, very occasionally, a Master will take on a pupil as a special disciple — but only after the pupil has undergone a long series of exhaustive tests in some menial position, after which the pupil would still have to ask to be accepted as a full trainee. The impulse always comes from the seeker, never from the

Master. When the goat is ready to become a tiger, the Master will show it where the water is; but it is still up to the goat to make the effort to open its eyes and to become aware of its real identity. No old tiger will force your eyelids open for you.

In some places, usually as an adjunct to an ashram, there are special schools set up to teach the philosophy of the Master, but these simply pass on the overall principles of that particular aspect of universal wisdom. The details of the 'special' skills are not part of the curriculum. These are held back to be passed on only to those who have reached the necessary level of overall Lattice purity. 'Purity' does not mean being 'holier than thou'. It simply means a level of understanding where the needs of humanity are more important than the needs of the personality. Masters and their special pupils are still human beings. They balance laughter and fun against times for seriousness and contemplation. They have favourite foods and watch television, but these things are for relaxation and no longer govern any part of their life. They have preferences but they do not have habits. In fact they are able to use their 'humanness' to help their overall awareness; and it does not cloud their ability to 'see' clearly.

Although many people would like the power of a Master, very, very few could live with the requirement of being totally unselfish. And if we look at motives for a moment, most people want power so as to feel more secure. They do not want to worry about having to pay the gas bill, but want to feel comfortable being the ones who tells others what to do. These motives negate the mastership criteria. Looked at another way, the main requirement for someone to step on to the mastership path is *trust*. Trust that 'all is very, very well': that whatever happens it is the correct thing to be happening at that moment, whether it feels pleasant or painful. This level of trust is not easy to attain and although many people say that they feel they are at that level, when it comes to the test they mostly find that there is a part of them either saying that 'it's not fair' or 'I'm worried about that aspect'. This is the personality still trying to take charge.

There are different levels of mastership. Some have finished the total course and have become fully fledged world teachers, such as Buddha or the Dalai Lama. Others still have part of the way to go and are classed as gurus, (teachers), or enlightened beings. The move from being an ordinary human with prejudices, fears and habits to the level of overall awareness that we call enlightenment is similar to the transition of a student from school to university. It is not the end of the road and a lot more awareness is still required. A general understanding of the way that the Lattice operates is now comprehended, although not necessarily in those terms, but many details still need to be learned before status of world teacher is attained. Some enlightened persons decide to move no further for the time being and remain at a given level in order to act as beacons for other seekers on the path. Others move to other parts of the galaxy where different types of instruction are available. Some cease to function at a human level for a while and supplement other energies of the Lattice. There are a great variety of situations ready to be filled and the point to remember is that the *eventual* finishing point, whatever line is taken, will be the losing of all unbalanced energies, the making of a 'reactionless' action, and a return to the originating Source residing in the Lattice gaps. Masters are aware of this as a reality; ordinary mortals only know it as theory.

Before moving on to discuss miracles and magic, consider the statement just made that some enlightened beings move to other parts of our galaxy. We all know the myths about the ancient gods, and tales about super-beings who supposedly helped with all sorts of Earth mysteries from the construction of the pyramids to the building of Atlantis. There will never be acceptable proof that such beings either did or did not exist. In more modern times, we have been made aware of UFOs and 'little green men from space'. These have largely been shown to be optical illusions, drunken visions, or wishful thinking. But a few of them have defied explanation and remain mysteries. If the theory of the Lattice structure is correct, there is no reason why beings who understand how the Lattice functions should not use its transmission capabilities to send holographic-type representations of themselves to distant places. Or in some cases, they might send the soul energy, (which is non-physical and can move faster than light), to be clothed in an appropriate body at the place of arrival. The primary purpose of these transfers would either be to help an emerging civilisation or to stop it from self-destruction.

It is interesting to note that the time of maximum UFO sightings was just at the time that the world seemed bent on atomic self-destruction. Once that danger was passed, the number of sightings diminished. There was never any need for 'little green men' to disembark from their flying saucers and say, 'Take us to your leader'. The purpose of the UFOs in the first place was simply to put healing energies into the world's aura. How the energies were used was always up to humanity. Just as patients won't regain full health unless they have a real wish to do so, so the healing energies supplied to the world will not produce a full cure unless humanity really wants it to be so. Although the danger of a nuclear holocaust has receded for the time being, we now seem bent on alternative destruction by pollution, so our unseen helpers are having to start work once again to make us more ecologically aware.

There are similar problems in other parts of the galaxy and masters from our world can help the beings in those distant parts to solve them. Where we have learned how to control electromagnetic forces, other worlds have learnt how to overcome population problems, and yet others are experts in horticulture. Just as there is a World Health Organisation to spread the results of medical research to all nations, so there are similar intergalactic cooperative efforts, using enlightened beings as their ambassadors. It seems a bit far-fetched if viewed from the conventional stance of Earth sciences; but viewed as part of the universal span of the Lattice, in which the speed of light is no longer a limiting factor, it is quite reasonable.

This brings us nicely on to the subject of magic because one of the intergalactic founders of Earthly magical sciences was a super-being known as Hermes Trismegistus, also known as Thoth or Hiram Abiff. Hermes Trismegistus was his Neo-platonic name and it means 'thrice greatest Hermes'. Thoth was the Egyptian name and it meant 'the Word' or Logos. And Hermes is Greek for 'messenger' or 'communicator'. Hiram Abiff was mentioned in the Bible as one of the helpers of King Solomon in the building of the temple at Jerusalem. He was supposed to be a master craftsman, especially with iron and brass. The likelihood is that he was a specialist in the manipulation of all materials, especially gold.

Apart from these attributes, Hermes was also the father of alchemy, which was the forerunner of all forms of magic. The word 'alchemy' probably comes from two Arabic words 'al' meaning 'the' and 'kimia' meaning 'art' or 'science'. Some schools of thought think that it is an Egyptian word meaning 'black' and the full word means 'the black art', but this is probably the result of magic later being associated with bad effects. The only thing we can be sure of is that the original art of alchemy eventually gave rise to the science of chemistry and the word embracing this discipline.

Because of its later associations with wizened old men muttering over bubbling retorts in dingy garrets, alchemy has had a bad press for many years. The original science was not for the production of gold, or for the elixir of life, but simply taken as one of the many paths to godliness. Hermes said that a true understanding of alchemy would lead the student to 'the greatest gift that it is possible to have'.

Materialistic man translated this to mean that he would end up with lots of gold, whereas the gift Hermes was talking about was perfection. He also talked about 'eternal life', (meaning a return to the Source), and this got degraded into the elixir of life, or perpetual existence as a human being.

The sad fact is that a partial understanding of the alchemical books can indeed lead to the ability to transform base metals, but the price for this misapplication is a heavy karmic debt which can take many life-times to correct. As is the case with all powerful tools, misuse can result in serious accidents and lots of pain and destruction.

It is always possible for any reasonably intelligent person to study a subject and then to misapply it. Look at the 'legitimate' frauds constantly perpetrated by clever financiers, and the subtle messages put out by advertisers who are psychologically aware. The same applies to alchemy. In essence, the science of alchemy is a full understanding of the four elements and their inter-relationships. Once a person is fully aware of the way in which the energies move between levels and the various bypasses that exist, all sorts of seemingly miraculous results can be achieved. But these results are only achieved at a price, and that price is that the instigator must be sufficiently isolated from the processes for none of the alchemical energy to leak across from experiment to experimenter. This means in practice that the experimenter *must not be emotionally involved* — an almost impossible obstacle for ordinary human beings. Those that try to harness the greater powers of alchemy almost invariably become corrupted because they are seeking self-gratification. This manipulation of the special forces of the universe may initially lead to wealth and power, but finally results in a heavy karmic debt which must be repaid. Not necessarily in the same lifetime — the soul carries its karmic balance sheet from life to life as was pointed out earlier.

This is the major difference between miracles and magic. Miracles help others, magic helps the self. Thus, miracles are pain-free while magic includes an inevitable built-in penalty. And because we have freewill, the decision is left to us, whether we wish to study this science and experiment with its various aspects.

It is worth remembering one or two of the principles upon which miracles are based. Firstly, miracles are basically altruistic. Secondly, everyone has the capability to perform them, (but they work better if the performer is a clear channel). Thirdly, a miracle is a service to others. The less attached to the outcome the miracle worker is, the more likely he or she is to be successful.

These three principles emphasise that true miracles are invariably directed towards other people and are not part of any process of self-gratification. Selfless love is the prime motivation. The second principle emphasises that, although we all have the capability of performing miracles, they will not work unless personality has been removed from the equation. If personality is there, magic may result, but not a miracle. The third principle reiterates that the pinnacle of humankind's achievement is to serve others. The snag is that, generally speaking, serving others *in order to reach that pinnacle* means that we are not really serving others but ourselves. In this case the action either doesn't work at all or it only functions at a lower level. True service is instinctive, not logical.

A fourth principle which is worth noting is that the prime energy of miracles is generated at the AIR level. Although all thoughts originate at the WATER, or desire, level, the energy for their operation comes from the mental realm. Thoughts can represent the lower or bodily level of experience, or the higher or spiritual level of experience. One makes the physical, and the other creates the spiritual.

This takes us back to the previous chapter where it was pointed out that all creativity comes from the mental plane, and it gives a clue to one of the ways of reversing the downward flow of energy from the spiritual to the physical.

Lower thoughts, that is those concerning the needs of one's own body and welfare, create physical patterns. Higher thoughts, that is those concerning the welfare of others, move the energy in the opposite direction, up from the mental to the spiritual level. It is also worth noting that, as movement upwards from the mental level takes us outside the constrictions of time, (which only exists as a concept of the logical mind), miracles transcend time and allow a re-arrangement of the accepted order of events. It takes time to get used to this concept, which is an essential part of many miraculous processes. Considered by the logical mind such time re-arrangements are an impossibility: how could a time-controlled mind possibly think otherwise? But taken into the higher realms beyond the mind, where time does not exist, the order of events is immaterial and A can follow B as easily as B may follow A. What we desire is what will happen.

The only item left for discussion in this chapter is the Akashic records. These are mentioned in a number of spiritual writings as the complete records of the path of each soul from initial incarnation; it also records the experiences of all other realms — animal, vegetable and mineral. They are said to be open for viewing and study by those people who who are able to exercise sufficient mind control and are no longer emotionally restricted. This is the same as saying that these records are the continuing Lattice vibrations at the mental level of all events which have ever taken place. We know that the vibrations and the nodal patterns continue to exist long after the initiating energies have moved on, so this picture of the mental plane known as the Akashic records fits well with the theory of the Lattice. As Masters are able to rise above their emotions they are able to browse in the Akashic Records at will. They don't do so without good reason because their general policy regarding other souls is one of non-interference. It is the private business of each soul to find its own path back to the Source. However, when a soul asks for help, the Master's ability to look at past lives and karmic debts is always available.

Ways of using all the information set out far so concerning the Lattice, mastership and the place of Cosmos within it will be discussed in the next and final chapter.

Chapter 14

The Way Forward

By now it should be clear that science and spirituality are not as far apart as many people imagine. They are held together and balanced within the structure of the Lattice. Scientists are not so much against spirituality as against things that can't be proved or demonstrated under controlled conditions. They prefer a world where logic rules, whereas much that takes place in the spiritual and paranormal worlds cannot be tied down to controlled experimentation.

However, the theory of the Lattice has given reasonable explanations for a lot of the events which appear at first sight to be unscientific, although they still cannot be taken into a laboratory and reproduced time after time. This will continue to be the case until some form of measuring instrument is designed which will replace the human part of the sensing system. Nevertheless, the Lattice system is compatible with general scientific facts and theories. It is in accord with both quantum theory and relativity; it accepts that light travels in waves, and the phenomenon of photon bundles; it obeys Newton's laws and all the other rules and observations of science.

Thus the idea of the Lattice does not go against the normal rules of science. Can the same be said for the unexplained phenomena of the universe and for spiritual experience? The chapters on miracles and ghosts showed that the Lattice can support these peculiar events too. Throughout the book it has been shown that the structure of the Lattice is compatible with spiritual experience. What now remains is to show how the knowledge gained thus far can be put to good use and become part of our everyday awareness of the world in which we live. Once this process is properly understood, we will be able to continue our journey back to the Source with increased awareness of the roses around us; we will also begin to see our tigerness in the pool of life's experiences.

As mentioned in chapter 1, we are, astrologically speaking, at the beginning of a new age — the Age of Aquarius. This is not the place to go into the pros and cons of astrology and it does not matter whether you believe in it or not. If you do, then you will already have thought about the implications of new age energies; if you do not, then just consider all the immense changes that have taken place in the last 200 years: the technical changes; the political changes; the financial changes; the changes in health awareness, in people-care, in international cooperation,and in community responsibility. These indicate a new level of world communication and overall human awareness, whatever title we give it. (The move from the age of Pisces to that of Aquarius is greatly concerned with replacing autocracy and oligarchy by systems involving greater community awareness and responsibility.)

From the point of view of the Lattice, this is a time when fundamental galactic energies are changing their resonances and are feeding new types of vibrational patterns to our planet. The Lattice has its own galactic and planetary resonances which occur independently of the more localised resonances concerned solely with worldly and human events. The origin of these resonances is what we call the 'Zodiac', a circle of twelve different energy sources far out in our galaxy. These special resonances reach a peak every 2,000 years or so and the rise and fall of the peak lasts for about 450 years. In astrological terms each 2,000 year period is called a Great Month, (or an 'Age'), and twelve Great Months form a Great Year, which lasts about 25,000 Earth years. This particular Age started moving towards its peak in about 1,750 AD and will run down again in about 2,200 AD. So we are right at the top of the peak at this end of the

20th century. This means in practical terms that we are in the middle of major changes at all levels. (Hence the exciting times we live in.) For those who are aware of these cosmic shifts, this is a busy and demanding time: a time to get things done; a time for major spiritual progress; a time when the planet is more open to speedy evolution. It is also a time of maximum discomfort for world inhabitants because major changes disrupt all levels of life.

Naturally, during these changes, humans will be experimenting with the new energy patterns and trying to understand them. Dependent on the 'personality content' (PC) of these experiments, they will either go on to enhance the major resonance, (if the PC is low), or to be a nine day's wonder if the PC is high. A look back through recent history already shows us these effects at work. Even major experiments such as communism have floundered because the administrators could not keep their need for personal power out of the equation. Similarly, major religions are undergoing important changes. Numerous alternative Christian sects are arising —fundamentalism; television evangelism; all the crusaders who come round knocking on doors at weekends; etc.). The Jewish religion has split into two parts: 'traditional' and 'modern'. Islam is in the throes of a major upheaval as fundamentalists war with more open sects. Buddhism sees new variants coming into being every few years. And so on. Religion is nearly always the first bastion to be knocked down and rebuilt when new ages come into being. (Zoroastrianism, Taoism, Confucianism and Jainism were all started between the 7th and 6th centuries BC; Christianity early in the first century AD. These changes all occurred during the run-up to the Piscean Age.)

So this is a special opportunity for each one of us to examine our individual spiritual progress and see if the new energies can help us find more enjoyment as we move along our path. We have each come into incarnation at this time especially to take advantage of this 'once in many life-times' opportunity, whether we remember our 'out of incarnation' decisions or not. A good working knowledge of the Lattice will help us to exploit this opportunity. Note that we are talking about *spiritual* and not *religious* progress. There is a big difference.

All religions are based on dogma — they have rules and regulations which need to be obeyed if their adherents are to be 'saved'. Within the religious teachings are the original inspirations of the founder but these are inevitably diluted by the requirements of the religion's administrators. Politics always creep in to satisfy the need for the priests to retain control of their followers. It is an unfortunate fact that the power wielded by those in high religious office is often more political and financial than spiritual. Churches, mosques and synagogues need to be paid for, heated, and kept in good repair; priests, mullahs and rabbis need to be clothed and fed; artifacts need to be kept in good condition and occasionally replaced. Thus, religions are of necessity part business enterprises, and part of the attention of the clergy has to be focussed on keeping the trappings of the religion in good order. This frequently means that the priests have to keep on the right side of local government and commerce. It soon becomes difficult for them to keep sacred and secular requirements separate.

On the other hand, spirituality is purely a matter between an individual and Cosmos. No intermediaries are necessary; no church or holy buildings are required; dogmas are not mandatory. Thus, no secular matters need impede the communication process. Spirituality is always a matter of trust; religion is usually a matter of security. (Book your place in heaven to avoid the fires of damnation.) Therefore, although religions contain a variable measure of spirituality, spirituality can exist independently of religion. In this book we are only concerned with aspects of spiritual progress. The true spiritual path is always somewhat frightening, until the first level of enlightenment is reached. On the spiritual path there is no-one to blame, no one to ask for mercy, no one to look to as a father/mother figure, no one who offers security. It is an *individual and solitary path*. But, in the end, it is the only realistic path that there is. All other paths are transitory, even though it takes us many hundreds of life-times to understand this.

A major purpose of this book has been to bring you, the reader, to a closer awareness of this fact. Descriptions of the Lattice, the existence of Cosmos in the non-space, non-time region between the strings, discussions on the points of difference and equivalence between science and spirituality, and all the rest of the contents of this book are simply there as guidelines to your own individual journey back to the Source.

Remembering the story in chapter one, there are a number of old tigers about, (Masters), who wander by every now and then to pick the odd cub out from the goats and carry it to the pool. But it is still up to the cub to overcome its fright, to open its eyes and *see*. Alternatively, we have to pluck up the courage to leave the herd voluntarily and risk being killed on the way to self-realisation. 'Killed' is an emotive word: we have all been killed or have died countless times and we know for certain that the same process will happen again. (This is assuming that we now believe in reincarnation). But our personality in this life whispers to us that *this* time will be different. *This* time we will live forever. It has to believe this as its very existence depends on our earthly vitality. The personality does not survive the death of the emotional-physical body, because that is where it lives. The soul, being made of less dense materials, does survive to form the core of our next life. Our personality makes us believe that this particular body matters more than as a simple vehicle for the soul to use in this incarnation. That is part of its job. And it does its work so well that we forget why we are here and think that we are just goats.

There is now no excuse for this self-deception any more.

At least, not if you have been paying a reasonable amount of attention while reading this book. This doesn't mean that you should now renounce your present lifestyle and join a 'New Age' community, or become a travelling holy person, or in fact make any startling changes to the way you live from day to day. What it *does* mean is that you will now begin to see things with a new awareness. You see the interconnectedness of all things. You see how the ripples at one point in the Lattice cause effects in entirely different places. You feel the godliness of all things. You don't necessarily have to *like* all things or all people. But you should be aware that they are a part of you and you are a part of them. Therefore you feel akin to them: you feel love for them. Not physical love, but spiritual love. There is a big difference. Physical love is ultimately based on a need for security and a need to possess. Spiritual love is quite selfless. It does not come and go like physical love. Once acquired, it stays. This doesn't imply that spiritually mature people go round embracing everyone and looking lovesick. But everyone and everything *matters* to them. It is an attitudinal rather than a physical change.

There are two or three methods of communicating directly with spirit. These have been used for thousands of years and are still powerful. They have all been mentioned before but are worth repeating. They all involve trying to reduce the activity of the logical mind so that our spiritual communication mechanism has a better chance of being heard. The first is meditation; the second is prayer; and the third is attunement.

There are lots of books available on meditation techniques. Some people find this one helpful; others prefer that one. The only way to find out is to try a few. The same, surprisingly enough, applies to prayer. Some people pray as though they were really *inferior*; others carry on a one-to-one conversation with God. Some people like to pray with others; other people prefer to communicate separately. Once again, there is no one way which is correct for all. If prayer is your way of communicating with spirit, try a few variations and see which are more comfortable for you. The way you were taught at school or church is not necessarily the best way for you now.

The third method — attunement- is something which can be applied on an everyday basis to practically any situation. It is the way a lot of communities work these days and it applies equally well to individuals. The purpose of attunement is to align oneself with the Lattice's energies before undertaking any task. The task does not have to be a big one. The objective is to be in resonance with one's surroundings so that the tasks are performed with more tranquillity and efficiency. Not only does this produce a better result; it keep one's body healthier and less prone to stress-related illnesses, and also is a sure way of increasing awareness. Furthermore, attunement is equally possible and appropriate in both boardroom and kitchen.

For an individual the process of attunement involves being silent for a few moments before starting any project. During that silence you imagine your connections with both the task to be done and all the unseen beings which are available to help you —angels, elementals, etc. See that you are connected with these forces, particular at the heart, head and solar plexus. Feel also your connection with the earth and with the energies coming from your personal angels. Acknowledge these presences as friends. Then start the project from a space of peace. The whole attunement process need take no more than 10-15 seconds, but it is well worthwhile.

The same process applies to groups, but in this case it helps for the people to hold hands in a circle, with the right hand facing up and the left down. (Or the other way round; the main point is for all in the circle to have the same hand pattern.) You can stand up or sit down, it doesn't matter which. And the circle doesn't need to be circular; it just needs to be a continuous connection. The heart, head and solar plexus energies can be imagined as circles of light connecting the group together. Sometimes it feels appropriate for someone in the group to say a few words, but this is not mandatory. After the short silence, one person signals the end of the attunement by squeezing the hand on each side and the 'squeeze' is passed round the circle as people let go. This group process works well as a start to anything: from a team doing the washing up to a collection of directors starting a board meeting. A peaceful energy is generated by it which makes the work that follows lighter, more enjoyable and more efficient.

The one thing to emphasise above all else in any process of self improvement and realisation is the keyword *awareness*. Don't let meditation, prayer or attunement become such an everyday affair that it becomes a 'non-feeling' automatic ritual. It is an easy state to fall into. Just listening to the time-worn prayers recited in hundreds of Christian churches shows that many priests and congregation members are murmuring the words while thinking about whether there will be time to pop into the pub before lunch. Awareness of the true meaning of the service has long gone. And the same can apply equally well to both meditation and attunement. Ritual is a useful tool to help us move quickly and smoothly into another state of consciousness, but we need to be aware of whether that state is currently beneficial. The purpose of ritual is to move us into the correct Lattice resonances so that more energy can be focussed on the job in hand. Therefore the resonances should include plenty of outgoing energy. The daydreaming rituals of bored priests and unfocussed congregations simply go into energy-consuming cycles, giving nothing out to benefit either the participants or the world. And the same can be said of tired attunement leaders, or of meditators who have let their periods of contemplation become excuses simply to 'switch off' from life for a time.

Awareness is a state of being present all the time. One of the supreme examples of this state is found in the Bible when Jesus, in the middle of ministering to a multitude of people, felt a sick woman touching his clothes so that she would be healed. There must have been dozens of people touching his clothes at that time because the Bible says that the multitude 'thronged about him' (Mark 5:24); but this one particular touch was different from the others because it was asking for a special energy. And Christ was immediately aware of it even though He was talking to a man with a sick daughter at the time. So He asked, 'Who touched my garments?' And His disciples could hardly believe their ears. 'Who touched your garments!' they exclaimed, 'Look at the multitude. How can you ask such a daft question. Dozens are touching you all the time.' But Christ was totally aware of this particular touch because it was so important to the sick woman; so he had her come forward and gave her a special blessing. (Mark 5: 25-34).

We cannot hope to have that level of awareness now, but we can at least hold onto it as something to strive for. It is a possible stage along the journey.

One possible classification of the main stages of the journey can be compared to the 'I am' milestones. This is an elementary exercise in self-awareness of which the point is to find a satisfactory answer to the question, 'Who am I?' At an early stage, the answer might be 'I am Ian Pullen', but this soon becomes inadequate because even if I were to change my name to Fred Bloggs I would still remain the same person inside. I am not just my name. Likewise I am more than what I do for a living; and I am more than my relationships with my family and other people.

So — who am I? Maybe the answer 'I am me' fits the bill. The 'me' encompasses my personality, consisting of my physical and emotional parts and my logical mind. But does it include my soul? The higher mind, buddhi and atma? I do not believe so, because the 'me' seems to be associated very strongly with personality patterns. 'I am me' serves mainly as a prop while I am growing up and during the period when my energies are concentrated in making the vehicle I use in this world strong and healthy.

Moving up through the elemental energies from AIR to WATER, an answer such as 'I am That' may be satisfactory. It moves the 'I' away from personality and into an acknowledgement of 'interconnectedness' and 'otherness'. I know that my feelings of separateness are actually false; therefore 'I am That'.

However, there are other energies beyond WATER — and the Journey goes right back to the Source. So how does FIRE play a part in this exercise? The standard answer is that the next stage towards the Source is the realisation 'I am That I am' which places me firmly at the higher monadic level in the whole Cosmic scheme. But this is still short of the ultimate target because, almost at the final milestone, the 'I' is no longer important. Separation is seen to be an illusion; and 'I' embraces everything and no longer has any relevance. Therefore the answer simplifies to a plain 'am'. At the target itself, the Source where timelessness resides, even the 'am' vanishes. Silence reigns and Cosmos is all.

Humanity tends to cling to its time-worn ways like old and well-loved shoes and won't consign them to the garbage heap even when they are no longer usable. It is simply fear of the unknown again. (Always our problems come back to fear.) Everyone is afraid: it is an instinctive animal state. A knowledge of the ultimate justice of karma and the workings of the Cosmic energies should help us to overcome the fear and to start taking risks. Over there, behind that menacing hill, may be just the mirror-surfaced pool we potential tigers have been looking for.

REMEMBER TO RELAX AND ENJOY
THE SCENERY ALONG THE WAY.

Introducing Findhorn Press

Findhorn Press is the publishing business of the Findhorn Community which has grown around the Findhorn Foundation, co-founded in 1962 by Peter and Eileen Caddy and Dorothy Maclean. The first books originated from the early interest in Eileen's guidance over 20 years ago and Findhorn Press now publishes not only Eileen Caddy's books of guidance and inspirational material, but many other books, and it has also forged links with a number of like-minded authors and organisations.

For further information about the Findhorn Community and how to participate in its programmes please write to: the Accommodation secretary, Findhorn Foundation, Cluny Hill College, Forres IV36 0RD, Scotland; or call +44 (0)1309 673655.

Here's a selection of books about the Findhorn Community...

THE KINGDOM WITHIN (£8.95)
A Guide to the Spiritual Work of the Findhorn Community
Compiled and edited by Alex Walker

This collection of writings about the history, work, beliefs and practices of the Findhorn Foundation and its associated community of spiritual seekers offers a vision of hope, inspiration and encouragement. With contributions by David Spangler, William Bloom, Dorothy Maclean, Peter and Eileen Caddy amongst others, this book covers topics which include nature and ecology, the art of living in community, the relationship of 'new age' thought to formal religion, and co-operation with the spiritual worlds. The world is hungry for the hope and inspiration this book brings — and so are you!

THE SPIRIT OF FINDHORN (£5.95)
by Eileen Caddy

This book offers a brief history of how Eileen gave up everything to follow her inner voice as well as sharing much of the guidance and wisdom which supported Eileen through the early days of her spiritual transformation and the birth of the Findhorn Community.

THE FINDHORN GARDEN (£9.95)
Pioneering a New Vision of Humanity and Nature in Cooperation
by The Findhorn Community

The story of the early days of the Findhorn Community and its communications with the nature kingdoms. Peter and Eileen Caddy's experiences as co-founders of the community, Dorothy Maclean's contact with the devas, R. Ogilvie Crombie's (ROC's) meetings with Pan and the Elemental Kingdom, and the wisdom of David Spangler and other combine to give a unique perspective on the relationship between humans and nature.

THE FINDHORN COMMUNITY (£8.95)
by Carol Riddell

The author traces the community's development over the years and gives a clear picture of the community today and the new businesses and independent projects springing up around it. The second half of the book includes a number of intimate and revealing interviews with members, both young and old, who share their lives and experiences of living in this incredible community.

For a complete catalogue, or for more information about
Findhorn Press products,
please contact :

Findhorn Press
The Park, Findhorn, Forres IV36 0TZ , Scotland
tel. 01309-690582 fax 01309-690036
e-mail thierry@findhorn.org